SLAVERY TIME
WHEN I WAS CHILLUN
DOWN ON MARSTER'S PLANTATION

INTERVIEWS WITH GEORGIA SLAVES

EDITED BY RONALD KILLION AND CHARLES WALLER

SLAVERY TIME WHEN I WAS CHILLUN DOWN ON MARSTER'S PLANTATION

THE BEEHIVE PRESS · SAVANNAH · GEORGIA

CONTENTS

INTRODUCTION

D URING the 1930's even the youngest former slaves were fast
disappearing from the American scene. These men and wom-
en were the last living witnesses to slavery in the United
States, and this was the final opportunity to learn from them what
slavery was really, intimately like. Field workers of the Federal Writers'
Project were dispatched throughout the Southeast, with instructions to
ask them about their birth, family, plantation life, the Civil War and
freedom, with specific questions about their parents' names and origins,
recollections of grandparents, living conditions, size of plantations and
number of slaves, food, clothing, housing, daily schedule, punishment,
slave sales, education, religion, runaway slaves, holidays, weddings,
funerals, patrollers, songs, superstitions, health and medicine, the coming of the Yankees, the Ku Klux Klan and life since the war. At the end
of the decade, more than ten thousand pages of typed manuscripts had
been deposited in archives, a rare personal record of life under slavery,
but one which has lain inaccessible and neglected for thirty years. This
volume is a selection of these interviews with former Georgia slaves.

Before the Civil War, recollections of former slaves who had made
their way to freedom in the North, Canada or England were published.
Few of these were about Georgia, for the road from Savannah to the

Canadian border was too long and hazardous for many successful escapes. Deplorable slave conditions described by the slaves themselves were the best argument against the institution of slavery, and Abolitionists used these reminiscences as propaganda. Many of the nineteenth-century confessions were entire or partial fabrications. Because of this tradition that they were factually unreliable, fugitive slave narratives of that sort were used only cautiously by historians and scholars.

After the Civil War, reminiscences of former slaves continued to appear, but they were neglected, for the social conservatism that swept the United States late in the nineteenth century contributed a form of racism to American scholarship. The plantation myth won, and the Negro was viewed as a charming, humorous, lovable, but rather ignorant, pathetic and unreliable figure, whose stories and tales about slave days were not to be taken seriously. The most influential study of slavery published in America during these years was Ulrich B. Phillips, *American Negro Slavery, A Survey of the Supply, Employment and Control of Negro Labor as Determined by the Plantation Regime*. The book presents a sympathetic view of slavery as a benevolent, paternalistic, civilizing system, and the author dismisses the slave narrative as an unreliable source for historical material.

The years following World War I saw a changing interest in Negro culture, however. Southern writers like William Faulkner and Eudora Welty found in the Negro a rich source for fiction; jazz and blues proudly proclaimed their Negro heritage; Harlem experienced its own cultural awakening; Negro folklore caught the popular imagination; and the expanding discipline of sociology saw in the Negro an authentic object for study. The social idealism which developed during the Depression stimulated a further concern for every class and condition of American life.

The Federal Writers' Project was created under the Emergency Relief Appropriations Act of 1935 to give jobs to unemployed writers, research workers and other qualified educated persons. With a sense of some urgency, since the last slaves were dying, the field workers of the Writers' Project began interviewing former Georgia slaves in 1936. But World War II abruptly ended the project. The original transcripts of the interviews were all deposited in the Library of Congress, whose collections do not normally circulate. The copies made for each state's files were haphazardly tossed uncatalogued into boxes to remain there while America went about its business of fighting war. Their relative inaccessibility is still another reason for the amazing neglect of these materials.

Now, finally, a reawakened interest in Negro studies has turned scholars back to the literature of slave narratives and reminiscences for sources of factual detail and essential understanding that can be found in no other place. E. A. Botkin's *Lay My Burden Down* (Chicago, 1945) is an entertaining selection from the slave interviews and remained the only published source of the Federal Writers' Project papers until Norman R. Yetman's *Life Under the "Peculiar Institution"* (New York, 1970), but in the entire book, Yetman used only five Georgia narratives. As this present volume shows, surely the Negro himself is the best source for Negro thought.

* * *

The slave on a Georgia plantation concerned himself with everyday survival as best he could. Life simply had to be lived, and the interviews collected here record that life. While the interviews certainly lend themselves to historical interpretation with complex social, psychological, cultural and literary value, they reveal most of all the plain truth that slavery was a human situation with human reactions, not an arbitrary,

[ix]

inflexible system of law and economics. Theorizing seldom occurred to the field hands on a Georgia plantation. They did not know they were living under any peculiar institution, nor were they consulted in the extensive religious, political and philosophical controversies about slavery.

These reminiscences reveal slavery as a basic accommodation between master and slave. Laws or movements had little influence on everyday plantation life. Each slave lived and worked under a system of benevolent despotism. Adjustments between master and slave were actually extra-legal, informal and varied. Although the slave codes of Georgia provided that slaves could not be taught to read, slave children were often educated by their masters and mistresses. Others even attended plantation schools. "Us had a white teacher," explains one slave, "and all he learned us slave children was just plain reading and writing." Georgia laws gave no legal sanction for slave marriages, but the rights of husbands and wives were generally secured. By law a slave could own no property, but any thrifty slave could lay up what he acquired, often from the produce of his small garden, and remain in secure possession. Some slaves even bought their freedom on the installment plan.

These interviews record a time and place which seem to have existed in a vacuum. Outside forces are seldom at work. The conditions of slavery simply depended upon the characters of both the slave and his owner. Legislators could deal with slavery as theoretically as they pleased. The slaveholders, year after year, day after day, often working beside their slaves in the fields, had to get along with them. Even though autocratic, cruel slave owners existed—one is described in this collection as "the meanest man in the world"—it was obviously to the master's advantage to be indulgent but firm. The slave's treatment depended most upon the character of the slave himself. If rebellious, the slave might be

flogged; if indolent or stupid, he might be sold to a trader; if disposed to render reasonable service, he was treated with consideration; if affectionate and faithful, he was likely to receive affection in return.

In their revelation of the public life of the slave, the interviews collected here seem disappointingly similar, but this is one point in favor of their reliability as factual documents. Slave life in Georgia remained very much the same in one place and in another, except for the minor differences dictated by climate, from the mountains in the north to the semitropical islands in the southeast. On each plantation, slaves were assigned regular work or trades, and life went on with little change as the same holidays were celebrated, the same crops harvested, the same food and clothing issued, the same work accomplished in season, the same prayer meetings and even the same superstitions passed from generation to generation.

It surprises us to find that these interviews, unlike the Abolitionist propaganda narratives published before the Civil War, are not uncompromising diatribes against the brutalities of slavery. They are not liberal sermons against man's inhumanity to man. Instead, they are the records of poor and simple former slaves, many of whom had found life uncertain and unprosperous in freedom, recalling a remote era when life was pleasant and their bodies were young. "You could hear Niggers a-singing in the fields 'cause they didn't have no worries like they got now," laments a former slave here. Most of the former slaves recall rivers filled with shrimp, oysters and fish, the swamps and pine woods teeming with wild turkeys, possums, squirrels, rabbits, deer and even wild boar. Change, even freedom, had become associated with worsening conditions. The Depression had not left Georgia when these interviews were made, and these poor, old and ill former slaves were feeling the heaviest effects of the hard times. "I don't find life so good in my

old age, as it was in slavery times when I was a child," one says here.

As factual documents, these interviews provide some fascinating footnotes to our knowledge of slavery. The everyday events of plantation living have never been so plainly stated. The brass-toed shoes, the troughs where the young children were fed with mussel shells for spoons, the wooden maple pegs which served as nails, the separate house for mammies and babies—these are the materials of these interviews, because they were close to the slaves. Marriages were performed by having the slave couple jump a broomstick, sometimes backwards. For dances musical bands were formed with buckets, pans and reeds as instruments. A cornshucking contest is described by one narrator, and another takes us to a wash day with lye soap and battling sticks. Where else but in these interviews can one discover the body lice which plagued Georgia in 1866, a legacy, according to the ex-slaves, of the Yankees.

These reminiscences are most appealing when describing, usually unintentionally, the subculture which developed among the slaves themselves—folk cures, folk songs, superstitions, slave religion and even a caste system. The real world of the slave differed from that which forced him to sweat nineteen hours a day (all the law allowed) under a hot Georgia sun. He lived an emotional and spiritual life quite separate from that of his master.

The slave's world existed without formal education or access to news beyond his own plantation. It is a world of superstitions and beliefs born in the slave's African heritage and nurtured through two centuries of slavery in America. Magic became a means of expression which his subculture demanded. In Georgia, as in other Southern states, the conjure doctor was an important plantation figure, a man or woman with remedies for all the troublesome aspects of life, an unrequitted love or an active enemy. He had love potions, magic concoctions for revenge or

[xii]

finding a hidden treasure, or foul-tasting medicines for inducing sleep or protecting against the evil eye. Devil's snuff, high john the conqueror root, lucky hand grass and graveyard dirt could be mixed in the right proportions to accomplish almost anything. For an aphrodisiac, a girl made for her lover a mixture of rabbit tobacco, sage, ginger and wahoo bark mixed with spring water. To cause an enemy to have a headache, the slave split a nut in two parts. When he crushed the nut, the enemy had a bursting pain in his head. However, the wise slave protected himself against conjure simply by carrying a buckeye in his pocket or sprinkling red pepper in his shoes.

Whereas the conjure doctor was often a malformed or mysterious creature, the plantation folk medicine expert was usually a black who had learned folk cures from a parent, practicing them on both slaves and master, usually with great success. The ex-slave narratives abound with prescriptions for the common ailments of life. To cure an earache, one snapped a betsey bug in half and allowed the blood to drop into the ear. An axe placed beneath the bed would cut off hemorrhage. If anyone had a fever, he could hang an onion in the room and the fever would enter it, but a solution of bruised peach tree leaves was also effective. For insect bites, a tobacco poultice was good; for respiratory ailments one drank fodder tea or the juice of wild plum bark.

The slave's world was a world caged by superstitions. If he dreamed of a snake, he was in danger; to dream of clear water meant good luck. Bad luck would follow him if he took up ashes after sunset or if a raven flew into his house or even if he brushed his hair after dark. Wood from a tree which had been struck by lightning could never be used for anything except fuel since it had been blasted by the hand of God. The slave watched for ghosts in graveyards and saw spirits in wells and trees. In her interview, one ex-slave recalls her meeting with the devil himself.

[xiii]

Slave subculture on the plantation even developed its own loose caste system. The common field hands were the lowest on the ladder since they had little contact with the master and were not specialists. The cooks and house servants were able to form a closer relationship with the white folks, so house service became a privilege, sometimes even a reward. The specialist slaves—blacksmiths, carpenters, brick masons—occupied a high social level and were in demand even in slave auctions where they always brought a higher price than field hands. The most privileged slave was the body servant, however, for he worked closely with his master and usually became his friend. He was the aristocrat of slave society.

Slave culture can be very clearly identified in religion. The churches which had the deepest influence relied little upon ritual and more upon spiritual and emotional reactions. The Baptists and Methodists achieved almost a monopoly on slave Christianity. "Everybody was Baptists then," says one ex-slave. But the formal worship service still belonged to the white man. When slaves attended, as they were required to do on many plantations, they received only the conservative line. "And that you are to serve your owners with cheerfulness, respect, and humility—not grumbling, or giving any saucy answers, but doing your work with readiness, mildness, and good nature; because sauciness and grumbling is not so much against your owners, as it is against God himself, who hath placed you in that service, and expects you will do the business of it as he hath commanded you." One former slave summarizes his reaction to the white man's Christianity: "The Blacks sat in the back of the church as the white minister preached and directed the following text at them: Don't steal your master's chickens or his eggs and your backs won't be whipped."

The real religion of the slaves was different. Interview after interview

speaks about secret services, bush arbor meetings or prayer meetings in the swamps. The same master who required attendance at Sunday service often punished with the lash those caught at these meetings. There the slave expressed his emotional reaction to "sweet Jesus," sang his spirituals which often speak of Heaven as the place of freedom and heard a rousing slave speaker. "Sometime on a plantation," explains a former slave, "a Nigger claim he done been called to preach, an' if he can get his master's consent, he can preach round under trees an' in cabins when it ain't work time." By some strange metamorphosis Solomon and Moses became blacks, and their exploits provided subjects for most black sermons. Moses above all other Old Testament figures was the hero who had freed the "Chillun of Israel from their bondage in Egypt." Incorporated in the slave interviews are puzzling and wonderful glimpses of slave beliefs which became part of slave religion. Lightning never strikes a sycamore tree because Christ blessed it. Ordinary springs originated from the steps of angels, or, if it is a bad spring, from the print of the devil's horses. Holes, caves and valleys are the result of an angel's hurling thunderbolts to earth; all splintered, shattered and cracked rocks and boulders were broken when Christ died.

During the decades of American slavery a system of morality developed which, while based certainly upon Christianity and the Protestant ethic, also contained other elements. Slave loyalty was often feudal. Many ex-slaves in their interviews recall with delight their success in saving the family livestock or silver from the Yankees who freed them. Most former slaves remained with their masters even after the war. Uncle Pierce, Alexander Stephens's personal body servant, followed him to prison.

Slavery was justified by a vague belief that the black would work better in the Georgia sun than could the white man. And work they did.

[xv]

It often accounted for the monotony and dreariness of life itself. But somehow working well became associated with Christian values, and the ex-slaves generally took pride in work. One comments that on the plantation, "The best thing they learned us was how to do useful work." The ex-slaves brag about their prowess in picking up to three hundred pounds of cotton a day, and they impress upon their interviewers how hard they've worked all their lives.

Life as a slave forced some moral accommodation even to Christian rules. If there was always plenty of food on a Georgia plantation, it was seldom meat, and most of the ex-slave interviews, while intoning against stealing, make an exception when it came to the master's smokehouse. Several former slaves even reveal the secret that meat, like a fresh shoat from the master's pen, was less traceable when boiled than when roasted, since there is little smell. One ex-slave recalls with delight, "A Nigger is just bound to pick up chickens and eggs if he can, no matter how much he done eat. He just can't help it."

The ex-slave narratives are most important in their unique access to the mind of the slave in the privacy of his life. Most slave histories have depended only on the written records of the slave owners or the white observer, both of whom saw a public slave. Only from one who lived under slavery can we ever find the answer to the question "What was it like to be a slave?" These interviews attempt to answer that question in a most personal way:

"Lots of girls were being sold by their masters who was also their father, taken right out of the yards with their white chilluns, and sold like herds of cattle."

"Sometimes we would sing if we felt sad and low down, but soon as we could we would go off where we'd go to sleep and forget all about trouble."

"They made me hoe when I was a chile and I'd keep right with the others, 'cause they'd told me if I got behind that a run-away Nigger would get me and split my head open and get the milk out of it."

"Grandma put her shoes in her pockets and when we got within a mile of the church she put her shoes on. . . . "

Finally, these narratives record attitudes as divergent as their narrators, and that is their greatest virtue. They depict human beings, not just types. Some are mean, dull and cowardly; others are courageous, compassionate and kind. Whatever they are, they are important because the slaves are allowed, finally, to speak for themselves.

* * *

The task of editing the manuscripts of the Federal Writers' Project interviews, now preserved at the University of Georgia, was formidable. It became clear that they required major cutting and selection. The interviews are sometimes damaged by errors of fact, inconsistencies, even contradictions. The workers who recorded the interviews often show their own personal prejudices and sympathies, which are sometimes condescending. The former slaves often flatter, exaggerate and tell what they think the interviewer wants to hear. Many of their "memories" are merely things told to them by older slaves, for when the first interviews were collected in 1936, the youngest former slave was already a septuagenarian and any ex-slave, even ten years old when freed in 1865, would have been in his eighties.

The editors were confronted with three major problems: (1) Selection. With over a thousand pages of typed manuscripts relating to Georgia, it was necessary to choose those which seemed most revealing, valuable and reliable. While remarkably few were ready for publication without change, almost all possessed information, sentiments or ideas

which we thought should be included. In even the weakest of the interviews there occasionally appeared a unique point important to slave history. Life is observed here from the viewpoint of the slave on the large plantation and the small, from the house servant and the field hand, from a contented slave and an oppressed one. In an Appendix we have grouped selections from further interviews to represent the total range of thought about certain subjects. This arrangement allowed the editors to include both the very best interviews in complete form, plus the very best portions of further interviews.

(2) Dialect. Most of the narratives are recorded in a heavy southern dialect, leading the unprofessional dialectitions of the Federal Writers' Project to numerous inaccuracies. Moreover, each field worker uses his own spelling for the dialect he records. Complex dialect often makes an interview almost unreadable. We have, therefore, changed spelling often, but never those more important aspects of language—style, diction and word order.

(3) Notation. In all cases, we have presented whatever information is available from the Federal Writers' Project Files: the names of the ex-slave and his interviewer and the place and date of the interview. We regret there is often so little.

meat, greens, syrup, cornbread, 'taters and the like. They catched plenty of possums and after they was kilt Ma would scald them and rub them in hot ashes and that clean't them just as pretty and white. They used to go fishin' and rabbit huntin' too. Us just fetched in game galore then, for it was the style them days. Seemed like to me in them days that ash-roasted 'taters and groundpeas was the best something to eat what anybody could want. 'Course they had a garden, and it had something of just about everything what us knowed anything about in the way of garden sass growin' in it. All the cookin' was done in them big old open fireplaces what was fixed up special for the pots and ovens. Ashcake was most as good as 'taters cooked in the ashes, but not quite.

Summertime, us just wore homespun dresses made like the slips they use for underwear now. The coats what us wore over our wool dresses in winter was knowed as sacks then, 'cause they was so loose fitting. They was heavy and had wool in them too. Marse Lewis, he had a plenty of sheep, 'cause they was bound to have lots of warm winter clothes, and then too, they liked mutton to eat. Them old brogan shoes was coarse and rough. When Marse Lewis had a cow killed they put the hide in the tanning vat. When the hides was ready, Uncle Ben made up the shoes, and sometimes they let Uncle Jasper help him if there was many to be made all at one time. Us wore the same sort of clothes on Sunday as evvyday, only they had to be clean and fresh when they was put on Sunday morning.

Marse Lewis Little and his wife Miss Sallie owned us, and Old Miss, she died long 'fore the surrender. Marse Lewis, he was right good to all his slaves; but that overseer, he would beat us down in a minute if us didn't do to suit him. When they give slaves tasks to do and they warn't done in a certain time, that old overseer would whip them. Marster never had to take none of his Niggers to court or put them in jails

[4]

RACHEL ADAMS

I WAS BORN in Putnam County about two miles from Eatonton, Georgia. My Ma and Pa was Melia and Isaac Little and, far as I knows, they was born and bred in that same county. Pa, he was sold away from Ma when I was still a baby. Ma's job was to weave all the cloth for the white folks. I have wore many a dress made out of the homespun what she wove. There was seventeen of us chillun, and I can't remember the names of but two of them now—they was John and Sarah. John was Ma's onliest son; all the rest of the other sixteen of us was gals.

Us lived in mud-daubed log cabins what had old stack chimneys made out of sticks and mud. Our old home-made beds didn't have no slats or metal springs neither. They used stout cords for springs. The cloth what they made the ticks of them old hay mattresses and pillows out of was so coarse that it scratched us little chillun most to death, it seemed like to us them days. I can still feel them old hay mattresses under me now. Every time I moved at night it sounded like the wind blowing through them peach trees and bamboos around the front of the house where I lives now.

Potlicker and cornbread was fed to us chillun, out of big old wooden bowls. Two or three chillun ate out of the same bowl. Grown folks had

[3]

SLAVERY TIME
WHEN I WAS CHILLUN
DOWN ON MARSTER'S PLANTATION

neither; him and the overseer set them right. Long as Miss Sallie lived the carriage driver drove her and Marse Lewis around alots, but after she died there warn't so much use of the carriage. He just drove for Marse Lewis and piddled around the yard then.

Some slaves learnt to read and write. If they went to meeting they had to go with their white folks because they didn't have no separate churches for the Niggers 'till after the war. On our master's place, slaves didn't go off to meeting at all. They just went around to one another's houses and sung songs. Some of them read the Bible by heart. Once I heared a man preach what didn't know how to read one word in the Bible, and he didn't even have no Bible yet.

There was hundreds of acres in that there plantation. Marse Lewis had a heap of slaves. The overseer, he had a bugle what he blowed to wake up the slaves. He blowed it long before day so that they could eat breakfast and be out there in the fields waiting for the sun to rise so they could see how to work, and they stayed out there and worked 'till black dark. When a rainy spell come and the grass got to growing fast, they worked them slaves at night, even when the moon warn't shining. On them dark nights one set of slaves held lanterns for the others to see how to chop the weeds out of the cotton and corn. Work was sure tight them days. Every slave had a task to do after they got back to them cabins at night. They each one had to spin their stint same as the womans, every night.

Young and old washed their clothes Sadday nights. They hardly knowed what Sunday was. They didn't have but one day in the Christmas, and the only difference they seed that day was that they give them some biscuits on Christmas Day. New Year's Day was rail-splitting day. They was told how many rails was to be cut, and them Niggers better split that many or somebody was going to git beat up.

[5]

About the most fun slaves had was at them cornshuckings. The general would get high on top of the corn pile and whoop and holler down leading that cornshucking song 'till all the corn was done shucked. Then come the big eats, the liquor, and the dancing. Cotton pickings was big fun too, and when they got through picking the cotton they ate and drunk and danced 'till they couldn't dance no more.

White folks just had to be good to sick slaves, because slaves was property. For Old Marster to lose a slave, was losing money. There warn't so many doctors them days and home-made medicines was all the go. Oil and turpentine, camphor, assfiddy [asafetida], cherry bark, sweetgum bark; all them things was used to make teas for grown folks to take for their ailments. Red oak bark tea was give to chillun for stomach miseries.

All I can recollect about the coming of freedom was Old Marster telling us that us was free as jack-rabbits and that from then on Niggers would have to get their own something to eat. It warn't long after that when them Yankees with pretty blue clothes on come through our place and they stole most everything our master had. They kilt his chickens, hogs and cows and took his horses off and sold them.

Interviewed at 300 Odd Street, Athens, by Sadie B. Hornsby.

GEORGIA BAKER

I WAS BORN on the plantation of a great man. It was Marse Alec Stephens' plantation about a mile and a half from Crawfordville, in Taliaferro County. Mary and Grandison Tilly was my Ma and Pa. Ma was cook up at the big house, and she died when I was just a little gal. Pa was a field hand, and he belonged to Marse Britt Tilly.

There was four of us chillun—me, and Mary, and Frances, and Mack. Marse Alec let Marse Jim Johnson have Mack for his bodyguard. Frances worked in the field, and Mary was the baby—she was too little to work. I was fourteen years old when the war was over. I swept yards, toted water to the field, and played around the house and yard with the rest of the chillun.

The long, log houses what us lived in was called shotgun houses because they had three rooms, one behind the other in a row like the barrel of a shotgun. All the chillun slept in one end room and the grown folks slept in the other end room. The kitchen where us cooked and ate was the middle room. Beds was made out of pine poles put together with cords. Them wheat-straw mattresses was for grown folks mostly because nigh all the chillun slept on pallets. However, there was some few slave chillun what had beds to sleep on. Pillows? Them days us never knowed what pillows was. Gals slept on one side of the room and

boys on the other in the chilluns room. Uncle Jim, he was the bed-maker, and he made up a heap of little beds like what they calls cots now.

Becky and Stafford Stephens was my Grandma and Grandpa. Marse Alec bought them in Old Virginny. I don't know what my Grandma done because she died before I was borned, but I remembers Grandpa Stafford well enough. I can see him now. He was a old man what slept on a trundle bed in the kitchen, and all he done was to set by the fire all day with a switch in his hand and tend the chillun whilst their mammies was at work. Grandpa Stafford never had to holler at them but one time. They knowed they would get the switch.

Marse Alec had plenty for his slaves to eat. There was meat, bread, collard greens, snap beans, 'taters, peas, all sorts of dried fruit, and just lots of milk and butter. Marse Alec had twelve cows and that's where I learned to love milk so good. George and Mack was the hunters. When they went hunting they brought back possums, rabbits, coons, squirrels, birds and wild turkeys. The same Uncle Jim what made our beds made our wooden bowls what they kept filled with bread and milk for the chillun all day. You might want to call that place where Marse Alec had our vegetables raised a garden, but it looked more like a big field to me it was so big. You just ought to have seed that there fireplace where they cooked all us had to eat. It was one sure enough big something, all full of pots, skillets, and ovens. They weren't never allowed to get full of smut neither. They had to be cleaned and shined up after every meal, and they sure was pretty hanging there in that big old fireplace.

Summertime us just wore what us wanted to. Dresses was made with full skirts gathered on to tight fitting waists. Winter clothes was good and warm; dresses made of yarn cloth made up just like them summertime clothes, and petticoats and drawers made out of osnaburg. Chillun

what was big enough done the spinning and Aunt Betsey and Aunt Tinny, they wove most every night 'till they rung the bell at ten o'clock for us to go to bed. Us made bolts and bolts of cloth every year.

Us went barefoot in summer, but us had good shoes in winter and wore good stockings, too. It took three shoemakers for our plantation. They was Uncle Isom, Uncle Jim, and Uncle Stafford. They made up holestock shoes for the womans and gals and brass-toed brogans for the men and boys. Holestock shoes had extra pieces on the sides so us wouldn't knock holes in them too quick.

Us had pretty white dresses for Sunday. Marse Alec wanted evvy-body on his place dressed up that day. He sent his houseboy, Uncle Harris, down to the cabins every Sunday morning to tell every slave to clean himself up. They warn't never give no chance to forget. There was a big old room set aside for a washroom.

Marse Lordnorth Stephens [cousin of Alexander W. Stephens] was the boss on Marse Alec's plantation. Course Marse Alec owned us and he was our sure enough master. Neither one of them ever married. Marse Lordnorth was a good man, but he didn't have no use for wom-ans—he was a sissy. There weren't no master no where no better than our Marse Alec Stephens, but he never stayed home enough to tend to things himself much because he was all the time too busy on the out-side. He was the President or something of our side during the war.

Uncle Pierce went with Marse Alec every where he went. His dog, Rio, had more sense than most folks. Marse Alec, he was all the time having big men visit him up at the big house. One time, out in the yard, him and one of them important men got in a argument about some-thing. Us chillun snuck up close to hear what they was making such a rukus about. I heared Marse Alec say: "I got more sense in my big toe than you got in your whole body." And he was right—he did have more

[9]

sense than most folks. Ain't I been a-telling you he was the President or something like that, them days?

Ma was Marse Alec's cook and looked after the house. After she died Marse Lordnorth got Mrs. Mary Berry from Habersham County to keep house at the big house, but Aunt Liza done the cooking after Miss Mary got there. Us little Niggers sure did love Miss Mary. Us called her "Mammy Mary" sometimes. Miss Mary had three sons and one of them was named Jeff Davis. I remembers when they come and got him and took him off to war. Marse Lordnorth built a four-room house on the plantation for Miss Mary and her boys. Everybody loved our Miss Mary, because she was so good and sweet, and there warn't nothing us wouldn't have done for her.

Marse Lordnorth never needed no overseer or no carriage driver neither. Uncle Jim was the head man what got the Niggers up every morning and started them off to work right. The big house sure was a pretty place, a-setting up on a high hill. The squirrels was so tame there they just played all around the yard. Marse Alec's dog is buried in that yard. I never knowed how many acres there was in the plantation us lived on, and Marse Alec had other places, too. He had land scattered everywhere. Lord, there was a heap of Niggers on that place, and all of us was kin to one another. Grandma Becky and Grandpa Stafford was the first slaves Marse Alec ever had, and they sure had a parcel of chillun. One thing sure Marse Lordnorth wouldn't keep no bright-colored Nigger on that plantation if he could help it. Aunt Mary was a bright-colored Nigger and they said that Marse John, Marse Lordnorth's brother, was her Pa, but anyhow Marse Lordnorth never had no use for her because she was a bright-colored Nigger.

Marse Lordnorth never had no certain early time for his slaves to get up nor no special late time for them to quit work. The hours they

worked was according to how much work was ahead to be done. Folks in Crawfordville called us "Stephens' Free Niggers."

None of Marse Alec's slaves never run away to no North, because he was so good to them they never wanted to leave him. The onliest Nigger what left Marse Alec's place was Uncle Dave, and he wouldn't have left except he got in trouble with a white woman. You needn't ask me her name because I ain't going to tell it, but I knows it well as I does my own name. Anyhow Marse Alec give Uncle Dave some money and told him to leave, and nobody never seen him no more after that.

Most times, when slaves went to their quarters at night, men rested, but sometimes they helped the womans card the cotton and wool. Young folks frolicked, sung songs and visited from cabin to cabin. When they got behind with field work, slaves worked after dinner Saturdays, but that wasn't often. But, oh, them Saturday nights! That was when slaves got together and danced. George blowed the quills, and he sure could blow grand dance music on them. Them Niggers would just dance down. There warn't no foolishment allowed after ten o'clock no night. Sundays they went to church and visited around.

Oh, what a time us Niggers did have on Christmas Day! Marse Lord-north and Marse Alec give us everything you could name to eat: cake of all kinds, fresh meat, lightbread, turkeys, chickens, ducks, geese and all sorts of wild game. There was always plenty of pecans, apples and dried peaches too at Christmas. Marse Alec had some trees what had fruit that looked like bananas on them, but I done forgot what was the name of them trees. Marse Alec would call the grown folks to the big house early in the morning and pass around a big pitcher full of whiskey, then he would put a little whiskey in that same pitcher and fill it with sweetened water and give that to us chillun. Us called that "toddy" or "dram." Marse Alec always had plenty of good whiskey, because Uncle

Willis made it up for him and it was made just right. The night after Christmas Day us pulled syrup candy, drunk more liquor and danced. Us had a big time for a whole week and then on New Year's Day us done a little work just to start the year right and us feasted that day on fresh meat, plenty of cake and whiskey. There was always a big pile of ash-roasted 'taters on hand to go with that good old baked meat. Us always tried to raise enough 'taters to last all through winter because Niggers sure does love them sweet 'taters. Us never knowed nothing about Santa Claus 'till after the war.

There warn't no special cornshuckings and cotton pickings on Marse Alec's place, but, of course, they did quilt in the winter because there had to be lots of quilting done for all them slaves to have plenty of warm covers, and you knows womans can quilt better if they gets a parcel of them together.

Old Marster was powerful good to his Niggers when they got sick. He had them seed after soon as it was reported to him that they was ailing. Grandpa Stafford had a sore leg and Marse Lordnorth looked after him and had Uncle Jim dress that poor old sore leg every day. Slaves didn't get sick as often as Niggers does now days. Mammy Mary had all sorts of teas made up for us, according to whatever ailment us had. The first thing they always done for sore throat was give us tea made of red oak bark with alum. Scurvy grass tea cleant us out in the springtime, and they made us wear little sacks of assfiddy around our necks to keep off lots of sorts of miseries. Some folkses hung the left hind foot of a mole on a string around their babies' necks to make them teethe easier.

I remembers just as good as if it was yesterday what Mammy Mary said when she told us the first news of our freedom. "You all is free now," she said. "You don't none of you belong to Mister Lordnorth nor Mister Alec no more, but I does hope you will all stay on with them,

because they will always be just as good to you as they has done been in the past." Me, I warn't even studying nothing about leaving Marse Alec, but Sarah Ann and Aunt Mary, they throwed down their hoes and just whooped and hollered because they was so glad.

Whilst Marse Alec was President or something, he got sick and had to come back home, and it warn't long after that before the surrender. Allen was appointed to watch for the blue coats. When they come to take Marse Alec off, they was all over the place with their guns. Us Niggers hollered and cried and took on powerful because us sure thought they was going to kill him on account of his being such a high up man on the side what they was fighting. All the Niggers followed them to the depot when they took Marse Alec and Uncle Pierce away. They kept Marse Alec in prison off somewhere a long time, but they sent Pierce back home before long. I seed Jeff Davis when they brung him through Crawfordville on the train. They had him all fastened up with chains.

I stayed on with my two good Marsters 'till most three years after the war, and then went to work for Marse Tye Elder in Crawfordville. I seed Uncle Pierce before he died and us sat and talked and cried about Marse Alec. Us sure did have the best master in the world. If ever a man went to Heaven, Marse Alec did. I sure does wish good old Marster was living now.

Interviewed at 369 Meigs Street, Athens, by Sadie Hornsby in August, 1938.

JASPER BATTLE

THEM DAYS before the war was good old days, especially for the colored folks. I know, because my Mammy done told me so. You see I was mighty little and young when the war was over, but I heared the old folks do lots of talking about them times whilst I was a-growing up, and then too, I stayed right there on that same place 'till I was about grown. It was Marse Henry Jones' plantation away off down in Taliaferro County, nigh Crawfordville, Georgia. Mammy belonged to Marse Henry. She was Harriet Jones. Daddy was Simon Battle and his owner was Marse Billie Battle. The Battle's plantation was off down there nigh the Jones' place. When my Mammy and Daddy got married Marse Henry wouldn't sell Mammy, and Marse Billie wouldn't sell Daddy, so they didn't get to see one another but twice a week: that was on Wednesday and Saturday nights, 'till after the war was done over. I can still remember Daddy coming over to Marse Henry's plantation to see us.

Slave quarters was log cabins built in long rows. Some had chimneys in the middle, twixt two rooms, but the most of them was just one-room cabins with a stick and mud chimney at the end. Them chimneys was awful bad about catching on fire. Didn't nobody have no glass windows. They just had plain plank shutters for blinds, and the doors was made

the same way, out of rough planks. All the beds was home-made and the best of them was corded. They made holes in the sides and foots and headpieces, and run heavy home-made cords in them holes. They wove them crossways in and out of them holes from one side to another 'till they had them ready to lay the mattress mat on. I've helped to pull them cords tight many a time. Our mattress ticks was made of home-spun cloth and was stuffed with wheat straw. Before the mattress tick was put on the bed a stiff mat wove out of white oak splits was laid on top of the cords to protect the mattress and make it lay smooth. Us was allowed to pick up all the old dirty cotton around the place to make our pillows out of.

Just a few of the slave families was allowed to do their own cooking because Marster kept cooks up at the big house what never had nothing else to do but cook for the white folks and slaves. The big old fireplace in that kitchen at the big house was more than eight feet wide and you could pile whole sticks of cordwood on it. It had racks across to hang pots on and big ovens and little ovens and big, thick, iron frying pans with long handles and hefty iron lids. They could cook for a hundred people at one time in that big old kitchen easy. At one time there was tables across one end of the kitchen for the slaves to eat at, and the slaves chillun ate there too.

Marster was mighty good to slave chillun. He never sent us out to work in the fields 'till us was almost grown up, say twelve or fourteen years old. Marster said he weren't going to send no babies to the fields. When slave chillun got to be about nine or ten years old they started them to fetching in wood and water, cleaning the yards, and driving up the cows at night. The biggest boys was allowed to measure out and fix the stock feed, but the most of us chillun just played in the creeks and woods all the time. Sometimes us played Injuns and made so much fuss

that old Aunt Nancy would come out to the woods to see what was wrong, and then when she found us was just a-having fun, she strapped us good for skeering her.

Mammy's job was to make all the cloth. That was what she done all the time—just wove cloth. Some of the others carded the bats and spun thread, but Mammy she just wove on so regular that she made enough cloth for clothes for all them slaves on the plantation and, it's a fact, us did have plenty of clothes. All the Nigger babies wore dresses made just alike for boys and gals. I was sure mighty glad when they allowed me to get rid of them dresses and wear shirts. I was about five years old then, but that boy's shirt made me feel powerful mannish. Slave gals wore homespun cotton dresses, and they had plenty of them dresses, so as they could keep nice and clean all the time. They knitted all the socks and stockings for winter. Them gals wore shawls, and their poke bonnets had ruffles around them. All the shoes was home-made, too. Marster kept one man on the plantation what didn't do nothing but make shoes.

Us never could eat all the meat in Marster's big old smokehouse. Sometimes he took hams to the store and traded them for sugar and coffee. Plenty of tobacco was raised on that plantation for all the white folks and the grown-up Niggers. Slave chillun weren't supposed to have none, so us had to swipe what tobacco us got. If our Mammies found out about us getting tobacco, they strapped us 'till the skin was most off our backs, but sometimes us got away with a little. If us seed any of the old folks was watching, us slipped the tobacco from one to another of us whilst they searched us, and it went mighty bad on us if they found out.

Slaves went to the white folks' church and listened to the white preachers. There wasn't no colored preacher allowed to preach in them churches then. They preached to the white folks first and then they let the colored folks come inside and hear some preaching after they was

through with the white folks. But on the big revival meeting days they allowed the Niggers to come in and set in the gallery and listen at the same time they preached to the white folks. When the sermon was over they had a big dinner spread out on the grounds, and they had just everything good to eat like chickens, barbecued hogs and lambs, pies and lots of watermelons. Us kept the watermelons in the creek 'till they was ready to cut them. A white gentleman, what they called Mr. Kilpatrick, done most of the preaching. He was from the White Plains neighborhood. He sure did try mighty hard to get everybody to obey the good Lord and keep his commandments.

Mr. Kilpatrick preached all the funerals too. When anybody died the first thing they done was to shroud them and lay them out on the cooling board 'till Old Marster's carpenter could get the coffin made up. There wasn't no embalmers them days and us had to bury folks next day after they died. The coffins was just the same for white folks and their slaves. On every plantation there was a piece of ground fenced in for a graveyard where they buried white folks and slaves, too. My old Daddy is buried down yonder on Marse Henry's plantation right now.

When a slave wanted to get married up with a gal, he didn't ask the gal, but he went and told Marster about it. Marster would talk to the gal and if she was willing, then Marster would tell all the other Niggers us was a-going to have a wedding. They would all come up to the big house and Marster would tell the couple to join hands and jump backwards over a broomstick, and then he pronounced them man and wife. They didn't have to have licenses or nothing like they does now. If a man married up with somebody on another place, he had to get a pass from his master, so as he could go see his wife every Wednesday and Saturday nights. When the patterollers catched slaves out without no passes, they evermore did beat them up. Leastways that what Mammy told me.

[17]

During the big war all the white folkses was off fighting except them what was too old to fight or what was too bad crippled and afflicted. They stayed home and looked after the womans and chillun. Somebody sent Mistress word that them Yankees was on the way to our plantation, and she hid everything she could, then had the hogs and horses driven off to the swamps and hid. Mammy was crazy about a pet pig what Marster had done give her, so Mistress told her to go on down to that swamp quick and hide that little pig. Just as she was running back in the yard, them Yankees rode in and she seed them laughing fit to kill. She looked around to see what they was tickled about and there following her like a baby was that pig. Them Yankees was polite like and they never bothered nothing on our place, but they just plumb ruined everything on some of the plantations right close to ours. They took nigh everything some of our neighbors had to eat, most all their good horses, and anything else they wanted. Us never did know why they never bothered our white folkses' things.

When they give us our freedom us went right on over to Marse Billie Battle's place and stayed there with Daddy about a year. Then Daddy come with us back to Marse Henry's and there us stayed 'till Old Marster died. Long as he lived after the war, he worked most of his help on shares, and seed that us was taken care of just like he had done when us all belonged to him. Us never went to school much because Mammy said white folks didn't like for Niggers to have no learning, but after the war was done over our Mistress let colored chillun have some lessons in a little cabin what was built in the back yard for the white chillun to go to school in.

Them was good old days. Us would be lucky to have them back again, especially when harvest time comes around. You could hear Niggers a-singing in the fields because they didn't have no worries like

they got now. When us got the corn up from the fields, Niggers come from far and nigh to Marster's corn shucking. That corn shucking work was easy with everybody singing and having a good time together whilst they made them shucks fly. The corn shucking captain led all the singing and he set right up on top of the highest pile of corn. The chillun was kept busy passing the liquor jug around. After it started getting dark, Marster had big bonfires built up and plenty of torches set around so as there would be plenty of light. After they ate all they wanted of them good things what had done been cooked up for the big supper, then the wrestling matches started and Marster always give prizes to the best wrestlers. There weren't no fussing and fighting allowed on our place, and them wrestling matches was all in good humor and was kept orderly. Marster wanted everybody to be friends on our plantation and to stay that way, for says he, "The Blessed Saviour done said for us to love our neighbor as ourselves, and to give and what us gives is going to come back to us." The Good Lord's words is always right.

Interviewed at 112 Berry Street, Athens, by Grace McCune in July, 1938.

JAMES BOLTON

MY PA was named Whitfield Bolton, and Liza Bolton was my Ma. Charlie, Edmund, Thomas, and John Bolton was my brothers, and I had one sister. She was Rosa. We belonged to Marse Whitfield Bolton, and we lived on his plantation in Oglethorpe County, near Lexington, not far from the Wilkes County line.

We stayed in a one-room log cabin with a dirt floor. A frame made out of pine poles was fastened to the wall to hold up the mattresses. Our mattresses was made out of cotton bagging stuffed with wheat straw. Our covers was quilts made out of old clothes. Slave womans too old to work in the fields made the quilts.

Ma went up to the big house once a week to get the allowance of victuals. They allowanced us a week's rations at a time. It were generally hog meat, corn meal, and sometimes a little flour. Ma done our cooking on the coals in the fireplace at our cabin. We had plenty of possums, and nobody asked us how we catched them. Slaves weren't allowed to have no guns and no dogs of their own. All the dogs on our plantation belonged to my master, and he allowed us to use his dogs to run down the rabbits. Nigger men and boys would go in crowds, sometimes as many as twelve at one time, and a rabbit ain't got no chance against alot of Niggers and dogs, when they light out for to run them

down. What wild critters we wanted to eat and couldn't run down we was right smart about catching in traps. We catched lots of wild turkeys and partridges in traps and nets. Long Crick runned through our plantation and the river weren't no far piece off. We sure did catch the fishes, mostly cats, perch and heaps of suckers. We catched our fishes most generally with hook and line, but the carpenters on our plantation knowed how to make basket traps that sure enough did lay in the fishes.

We didn't have no gardens of our own around our cabins. My master had one big garden for our whole plantation, and all his Niggers had to work in it whenever he wanted them to; then he give them all plenty good stuff for themselves. They was collards and cabbage and turnips and beets and peas and beans and onions, and they was always some garlic for ailments. Garlic was mostly to cure worms. They roasted the garlic in the hot ashes and squeezed the juice out of it and made the chilluns take it. Sometimes they made poultices out of garlic for the pneumony.

We saved a heap of bark from wild cherry and poplar and black haw and slippery elm trees, and we dried out mullein leaves. They was all mixed and brewed to make bitters. Whenever a Nigger got sick, them bitters was good for what ailed him. We took them for rheumatiz, for fever and for the misery in the stomach and for most all sorts of sickness. Red oak bark tea was good for sore throat.

I never seed no store-bought clothes 'till long after freedom done come. One slave woman done all the weaving in a separate room, called the loom house. The cloth was dyed with home-made coloring. They used indigo for blue, oak bark for brown, green husks often for black, and sumacs for red, and they'd mix these colors to make other colors. Other slave womans learned to sew, and they made all the clothes. Even during the summer time, we just wore shorts and pants made out of

[21]

plain cotton cloth. They wove some wool in with the cotton to make the cloth for our winter clothes. The wool was raised right there on our plantation. We had our own shoemaker man. He was a slave named Buck Bolton, and he made all the shoes the Niggers on our plantation wore.

When slaves got married, they just laid down the broom on the floor and the couple joined hands and jumped backwards over the broomstick. I done seen them married that way many a time. Sometimes my master would fetch Mistress down to the slave quarters to see a wedding. If the slaves getting married was house servants sometimes they married on the back porch or in the back yard at the big house, but plantation Niggers, what was field hands, married in their own cabins. The bride and groom just wore plain clothes, because they didn't have no more.

When one of the young masters and mistresses at the big house got married, they allowed the slaves to gather on the porch an peep through the windows at the wedding. Most generally they'd give the young couple a slave or two to take with them to their new home. My master's chilluns was too young to get married before the war was over.

My master and my mistress, they was sure all right white folks. I don't know much about the big house, because I was a plantation Nigger and I weren't no house servant. I remembers they lived in the big house. It was all painted brown. I heared tell they was more than nine hundred acres in our plantation, and lots of folkses lived on it. The biggest portion was woods.

We had one overseer at a time, and he always lived at the big house. The overseers weren't quality white folkses like our master and mistress, but we never heard nothing about no poor white trash in them days, and if we had heard something like that, we would of knowed better than to let Marster hear us make such talk. Marster made us call his overseer "Mister." We had one overseer named Mr. Andrew Smith,

and another time we had an overseer named Mr. Pope Short. Overseers was just there on the business of getting the work done. They seed after everybody doing his work according to order.

My master never allowed no overseer to whip none of his Niggers. Marster done all the whipping on our plantation himself. He never did make no big bruises and he never drawed no blood, but he sure could burn them up with that lash. Niggers on our plantation was whipped for laziness mostly. Next to that, whippings was for stealing eggs and chickens.

I weren't nothing but a child when freedom come, and in slavery time, chilluns weren't allowed to do no work, because the masters wanted their Niggers to grow up big and strong and didn't want them stunted none. That's how I didn't get no more beatings than I did. My master never give me but one licking. He had done told me to watch the cows and keep them in the pasture. I catched lots of grasshoppers and started fishing in the crick running through the pasture, and first thing I knows the overseer was rounding up all the other Niggers to get the cows out of the corn fields. I knows then, my time is done come.

Now and then a slave would run away and go in the woods and dig dens and live in them. Sometimes they run away on account of cruel treatment, but most of the time they run away cause they just didn't want to work and want to lazy around for a spell. The masters always put the dogs after them an get them back. They had black and brown dogs called Nigger hounds what weren't used for nothing but to track down Niggers.

The overseer woke up at sunrise and got us up. We would finish our victuals and be in the fields ready for work before many of us could even see the sun. We laid off work at sunset, and they didn't drive us hard at work. I done heard they was mighty hard on them on other plantations. My master never did allow his Niggers to work after sundown.

[23]

I never knowed Marster to sell but one slave, and he just had bought her from the market at New Orleans. She say it lonesome off on the plantation, and she asked Marster for to sell her to folks living in town. After he done sold her, every time he got to town she beg him to buy her back, but he didn't pay her no more attention. When they had sales of slaves on the plantations, they let everybody know what time the sale going to be. When the crowd get together they put the Niggers on the block an sell them. Leastwise they call it putting them on the block. They just fetched them out and show them and sell them.

There weren't no church for Niggers on our plantation, and we went to the white folkses church and listened to the white preachers. We set behind a partition. Sometimes on a plantation a Nigger claim he done been called to preach, and if he can get his master's consent, he can preach around under trees and in cabins when it ain't work time. These Nigger preachers in slavery time was called "cheerbackers." There weren't no cheerbackers allowed for to baptize none of Marster's Niggers. White preachers done our baptizing in Long Creek. When we went to be baptized they always sung, "Amazing Grace, How Sweet the Sound."

When folkses on our plantation died, Marster always let many of us as wanted to go lay off work 'till after the burying. Sometimes it were two or three months after the burying before the funeral sermon was preached. Right now I can't recollect no song we sung at funerals except, "Hark from the Tombs a Doleful Sound."

We visited around each others cabins at night. After supper we used to gather around and knock tin buckets and pans. We beat them like drums. Some used their fingers, and some used sticks for to make the drum sounds and most always somebody blowed on quills. Quills was a row of whistles made out of reeds or sometimes they made them out of

bark. Every whistle in the row was a diffunt tone, and you could play any kind of tune you wants if you had a good row of quills. They sure did sound sweet.

Spring plowing and hoeing times we worked all day Saturdays, but generally we laid off work at twelve o'clock Saturday. That was dinner time. Saturday night we played and danced, sometimes in the cabins and sometimes in the yards. If we didn't have a big stack of fat kindling wood lit up to dance by, sometimes the man and womans would carry torches of kindling wood whilst they danced, and it sure was a sight to see. We danced the "Turkey Trot" and "Buzzard Lope," and how we did love to dance the "Mary Jane." We would get in a ring and when the music started we would begin working our foots while we sung, "You steal my true love, an' I steal your'en."

We never did no work on Sundays on our plantation. The church was about nine miles from the plantation and we all walked there. Anybody too old and feeble to walk the nine miles just stayed home, because Marster didn't allow his mules used none on Sunday. All along the way the Niggers from other plantations would join us, and sometimes fore we get to the church house, they would be forty or fifty slaves coming along the road in a crowd. Preaching genully lasted till about three o'clock. In summer time we had dinner on the ground at the church. Everybody cooked enough on Saturday and fetched it in baskets.

Christmas we always had plenty good something to eat, and we all got together and had lots of fun. We runned up to the big house early Christmas morning and holler out, "Morning, Christmas Gift!" Then they give us plenty of Santy Claus, and we would go back to our cabins to have fun 'till New Year's Day. We knowed Christmas was over and gone when New Year's Day come, because we got back to work that day after frolicking all Christmas week. We would sing and pray Easter

[25]

Sunday and on Easter Monday we frolicked and danced all day long.

About the most fun we had was at corn shuckings, where they put the corn in long piles, and call in the folkses from the plantations nigh around to shuck it. Sometimes four or five hundred head of Niggers would be shucking corn at one time. When the corn all done been shucked, they'd drink the liquor the masters give them and then frolic and dance from sundown to sunup. We started shucking corn about dinner time and tried to finish by sundown so we could have the whole night for frolic. Some years we would go to ten or twelve corn shuckings in one year.

I ain't never forget when Mistress died. She had been so good to every Nigger on our plantation. When we got sick, Mistress always had us tended to. The Niggers on our plantation all walked to church to hear her funeral sermon, and then walked to the graveyard for the burying. It never was the same on our plantation after we had laid Mistress away.

We didn't know nothing about games to play. We played with the white folks' chilluns and watched after them, but most of the time we played in the creek what runned through the pasture. Nigger chilluns was always scared to go in the woods after dark. Folks done told us Raw Head and Bloody Bones lived in the woods and get little chilluns and eat them up, if they got out in the woods after dark.

My master didn't have no bell. He had them blow bugles for to wake up his hands and to call them from the fields. Sometimes the overseer blowed the bugle. If nobody else at the house the cook blowed it. Mistess done learned the cook to count the clock. None of the rest of our Niggers could count the clock.

One mornin' Marster blowed the bugle his own self and called us all up to the big house yard. He told us, "You all just as free as I is. You are

free from under the taskmarster, but ain't free from labor. You gotter labor and work hard, if you aims to live and eat and have clothes to wear. You can stay here and work for me or you can go where-some-ever you please." He said he would pay us what was right and, it's the truth, they didn't nary Nigger on our plantation leave our Marster then.

I worked on with Marster for forty years after the war. Right soon after the war we saw plenty of KuKluxers, but they never bothered nobody on our plantation. They always seemed to be having heaps of fun. Of course they did have to straighten out some of them brash young Nigger bucks on some of the other farms around about. Most of the Niggers the KuKluxers got after was on no farm but was just roaming around talking too much and making trouble. They had to take them in hand two or three times for some of them fool, free Niggers could be learned to behave themselves. But them KuKluxers kept on after them 'till they learned they just got to be good if they expect to stay around here.

It was about forty years after the war before many Niggers begun to own their own land. They didn't know nothing and it take them a long time to learn how to buy and sell and take care of what they makes. And heaps of Niggers ain't never learned nothing about things yet.

Now, I going to tell you the truth: now that it's all over I don't find life so good in my old age, as it was in slavery time when I was chillun down on Marster's plantation. Then I didn't have to worry about where my clothes and my something to eat was coming from, or where I was going to sleep. Marster took care of all that. Now, I ain't able for to work and make a living, and it's sure mighty hard on this old Nigger.

Interviewed at Athens by Sarah Hall in 1937.

SALLY BROWN

I WAS BORN four miles from Commerce, Georgia, and was thirteen years old at surrender. My mamma belonged to the Nash family—three old maid sisters—and my papa belonged to General Burns who was an officer in the war. There was six of us chilluns: Lucy, Nelvina, Johnnie, Callie, Joe and me. We didn't stay together long. I was give away when I was just a baby, and I never did see my mamma again. The Nashes didn't believe in selling slaves. If they got rid of any, it was giving them away. They sold one once because the other slaves said they was gonna kill him because he had a baby by his own daughter. So to keep him from being killed they sold him.

I was give to the Mitchell family, and they done everything mean to me they could. I was put to work in the fields when I was five year old, picking cotton and hoeing. And I slept on the floor nine years, winter and summer, sick or well. I never wore nothing but a cotton dress and my shimmy and drawers. I had such a hard time. That Mistress Mitchell didn't care what happened to us. Sometimes she would walk us to church, but we never went nowhere else. That woman took delight in selling slaves. She used to lash us with a cow-hide whip. When she died I went from one family to another. All the owners was pretty much the same.

They didn't mind the slaves mating, but they wanted their Niggers to marry only amongst them on their place. They didn't allow them to mate with other slaves from other places. When the women had babies they was treated kind and they let them stay in. We called it "layin-in". We didn't go to no hospitals. We just had our babies and had a granny to catch them. The granny would put a rust piece of tin or an axe under the straw tick, and this would ease the pains. Us didn't have no mattresses in them days but filled a bed tick with fresh straw after the wheat was thrashed, and it was good sleeping, too. Well, the granny put an axe under my straw tick once. This was to cut off the after-pains and it sure did too. We'd set up the fifth day and after the "layin-in" time was up we was allowed to walk out doors and they told us to walk around the house just once and come in the house. This was to keep us from taking a relapse.

We wasn't allowed to go around and have pleasure. We had to have passes to go wherever we wanted. When we'd get out there was a band of white men call the "patty rollers." They'd come in and see if all us had passes and if they found any who didn't have a pass he was whipped, given fifty or more lashes. And they'd count them lashes. If they said a hundred, you got a hundred. They was something like the Ku Klux. We was afraid to tell our masters about the patty rollers because we was scared they'd whip us again so we was told not to tell. They'd sing a little ditty. I wish I could remember the words, but it went something like this: "Run, Niggah, run, de patty rollers'll get you, Run, Niggah, run, you'd bettah get away."

Slaves was treated in most cases like cattle. A man went about the country buying up slaves like buying up cattle and the like, and he was called a speculator; then he'd sell them to the highest bidder. Oh! it was pitiful to see chillun took from their mother's breast, mothers sold, hus-

bands sold from wives. One woman he was to buy had a baby, and, of course, the baby come before he bought her and he wouldn't buy the baby; said he hadn't bargained to buy the baby too, and he just wouldn't. My uncle was married but he was owned by one master and his wife was owned by another. He was allowed to visit his wife on Wednesday and Saturday. That was the onliest time he could get off. He went on Wednesday and when he went back on Saturday his wife had been bought by the speculator and he never did know where she was.

I worked hard always. You can't imagine what a hard time I had. I split rails like a man. I used a huge axe made out of wood and an iron wedge drove into the wood, and this would split the wood. I helped spin the cotton into thread for our clothes. The thread was wound on big broaches—four broaches made four cuts or one hank. After the thread was spun we used a loom to weave the cloth. My mistress had a big silver bird. She would always catch the cloth in the bird's bill, and this would hold it for her to sew.

I worked from sun up to sun down. We never had overseers like some of the slaves. We was give so much work to do in a day and if the white folks went off on a vacation they would give us so much work to do while they was gone, and we better have all of it done too when they'd come home. Some of the white folks was very kind to their slaves. Some didn't believe in slavery and some freed them before the war and even give them land and homes. Some would give the Niggers meal, lard, and things like that. They made me hoe when I was a child and I'd keep right up with the others, because they'd tell me if I got behind that a run-a-way Nigger would get me and split my head open and get the milk out of it. Of course I didn't know then that wasn't true. I believed everything they told me and that made me work the harder.

There was a white man, Mister Jim, that was very mean to the slaves. He'd go around and beat them. He'd even go to the little homes, tear down the chimneys and do all sorts of cruel things. The chimneys was made of mud and straw and sticks. They was powerful strong too. Mister Jim was just a mean man, and when he died we all said God got tired of Mister Jim being so mean and killed him. When they laid him out on the cooling board, everybody was setting around, moaning over his death, and all of a sudden Mister Jim rolled off the cooling board, and such a running and getting out of that room you never saw. We said Mister Jim was trying to run the Niggers, and we was afraid to go about at night. I believed it then. Now I know that must have been gas and he was purging, for they didn't know nothing about embalming then. They didn't keep dead folks out of the ground long in them days.

Doctors wasn't so plentiful. They'd go around in buggies and on horses. Them that rode on a horse had saddle pockets just filled with little bottles and lots of them. He'd try one medicine and if it didn't do no good he'd try another until it did do good, and when the doctor went to see a sick person he'd stay right there until he was better. We used herbs a lot in them days. When a body had dropsy we'd set him in a bath made of mullein leaves. There was a jimson weed we'd use for rheumatism, and for asthma we'd use tea made out of chestnut leaves. We'd get the chestnut leaves, dry them in the sun just like tea leaves and we wouldn't let them leaves get wet for nothing in the world while they was drying. We'd take poke salad roots, boil them, and then take sugar and make a syrup. This was the best thing for asthma. It was known to cure it too. For colds and such we used ho-hound; made candy out of it with sorghum molasses. We used a lots of rock candy and whiskey for colds too. They had a remedy that they used for consumption: take dry cow manure, make a tea of this and flavor it with mint and give it

to the sick person. We didn't need many doctors then, for we didn't have so much sickness in them days, and naturally they didn't die so fast. Folks lived a long time then. They used a lot of peach tree leaves too for fever, and when the stomach got upset we'd crush the leaves, pour water over them, and wouldn't let them drink any other kind of water 'till they was better. I still believes in them old home-made medicines, too, and I don't believe in so many doctors.

We didn't have stoves plentiful then, just ovens we set in the fireplace. I has toted many a armful of bark, good old hickory bark to cook with. We'd bake light bread, both flour and corn. The yeast for this bread was made from hops. Coals of fire was put on top of the oven and under the bottom, too. Everything was cooked on coals from a wood fire, coffee and all. Once there was a big pot setting on the fire, just boiling away with a big roast in it. As the water boiled, the meat turned over and over, coming up to the top and going down again. Old Sandy, the dog, come in the kitchen. He sat there awhile and watched the meat roll over and over in the pot, and all of a sudden he grabbed at that meat and pulls it out of the pot. Of course he couldn't eat it because it was hot and they got the meat before he ate it. The kitchen was away from the big house, so the victuals was cooked and carried up to the house. I'd carry it up myself. We wasn't allowed to eat all the different kinds of victuals the white folks ate, and one morning when I was carrying the breakfast to the big house we had waffles that was a pretty golden brown and piping hot. They was a picture to look at and I just couldn't keep from taking one, and that was the hardest waffle for me to eat before I got to the big house I ever saw. I just couldn't get that waffle down because my conscience whipped me so.

They taught me to do everything. I used battling blocks and battling sticks to help clean the clothes when we was washing. We took the

clothes out of the suds, soaped them and put them on the block and beat them with the battling stick, which was made like a paddle. On wash days you could hear them battling sticks pounding every which-away. We made our own soap; used old meat and grease, and poured water over wood ashes, which was kept in a rack-like thing, and the water would drip through the ashes. This made strong lye. We used a lot of such lye, too, to boil clothes with.

Sometimes the slaves would run away. Their masters was mean to them and that caused them to run away. Sometimes they'd live in caves. How'd they get along? They got along all right—what with other folkses slipping things in to them. And then they'd steal hogs, chickens and anything else they could get their hands on. Some white people would help, too, for there was some white people who didn't believe in slavery. Yes, they'd try to find them slaves that run away and if they was found they'd be beat or sold to somebody else. My grandmother run away from her master.

I stayed with the Mitchells 'till Miss Hannah died. I even helped to lay her out. I didn't have a home after she died and I wandered from place to place, staying with a white family this time and then a Nigger family the next time. I didn't know about surrender and that I was free 'till after Miss Hannah died and I got out on my own. Lots of the owners didn't tell their slaves they was freed, and so we went right on working like we had been before the surrender.

Interviewed by Geneva Tonsell in Atlanta, June, 1939.

CICELY CAWTHON

I THINK I was about five or six, but I can remember nearly every-thing that went on about the last of the war. I was one of Marster's born slaves, but my father come from Charleston, South Carolina. He was sold to my master. He paid $1,000 for both him and his mother together. My daddy come out of the drove. His name was Charlie Hames, and he was what you call the butler now. He tended around the house. He never did go to the field. He drove the carriage too. My mother's name was Harriet. She was a house girl. She had nine boys and two girls. My mother was raised there on the plantation. Marster's father raised my mother. She was one of his born slaves. My mother's mother was the cook; Icie was her name.

Marster had three chillun. There was Miss Lula and Mr. Henry and one other; it died, just two living, that come to be grown.

Only thing I can remember when the Yankees come and told us we was free. Yankees had on blue coats and brass buttons. Why honey, them buttons shined like a gold dollar, all up and down, and we said, "How pretty them buttons are!" We had a smokehouse as big as my house and hams just piled up. The Yankees took all that from my Mistis. They took our carriage away too.

Marster had one of them big houses. It was pretty and white, so

white. Everything about it was white. Big two-story house, and two great big hickory trees hung right out over the kitchen. It was pretty, too. The dairy was under one of the hickory trees and the kitchen under the other. That was a shade for the kitchen, where us chillun could get out and play.

Everything inside of Marster's house was mahogany. They had curtains around the beds, tall beds, with them high posts. That's all the kind of beds they had, except little trundle beds you could slip up under the big bed in the daytime, pull it out at night and put the chillun to sleep. All the dishes was flowered. I don't know as I ever saw a plain plate, except in the quarters. They had blue and yellow flowered plates, cups and saucers flowered, too, and great big, long, covered dishes to match. There was great big goblets they used for everyday. They held about three cups. Mistis had a set of fine glass she hardly ever used except for mighty special company. Mighty special company had to come fore you could go in the sideboard and get them, because they was easy broke. That big sideboard, um! mahogany, the finest thing!

Our kitchen was off from the big house. I never saw such a big fireplace. The sticks of wood for that fireplace was twelve feet long. There was two big hooks up in the chimney. I've seen them hang lambs' and calves' hind quarters up in that chimney to smoke. They'd kill more than they could eat and didn't have ice to keep things from spoiling, so they hung them up in that chimney to smoke, how good! The sweetest stuff you ever ate in your life!

I know Marster had close onto a hundred slaves. Oh! he had the darkies! He had darkies there I didn't know nothing about. Cabins? Must have had about fifty cabins in the quarters. Darkies slept on straw mattresses, all of them. Of course they had plenty of quilts and cover. When they threshed every year, they throwed that old straw out and

put new straw in. Them log cabins was clean: they didn't have no chinches. The logs was fixed with mud. Mud was made up after the cabin was built and packed in the chinks, and when that got hard no wind couldn't get you. Sticks and mud was used to build the chimneys too.

They allowanced slaves their rations once a week. Great big smokehouse! It was something to see all the victuals that come from that smokehouse once a week—syrup, meal, flour, and bacon, a big hunk if there was a big family. Slaves didn't have cows, but there was plenty of cows on the place. Every darkey would bring his cup to the dairy and get milk, great big things, like measuring cups, they'd hold from a quart to a half a gallon. Slaves could get vegetables. Every colored family had a little place near their cabin to raise vegetables on if they wanted to. They didn't get no coffee; they drank milk. Nobody except the old women drunk coffee.

They had a passel of old women, about a dozen or two of them, that stayed in the house and minded the chillun while the others went to the fields. They had cradles they laid them in and little ticks for the cradles. Them ticks was made and dyed at home. Some of them was blue and some what you might call clay color. That was all them old women had to do, and they had better take good care of them babies. They was careful, just as careful of you as a breed sow, if you was going to have chillun, but they'd sell you off if you didn't have any.

Darkey womens wore white and blue striped dresses, spun and wove. Them that lived in the quarters had looms and reels. They spun their own cloth and made their own clothes. They made everything they wore except shoes. Uncle Jeff Hames, the shoemaker made all of the shoes that all of them wore on the place. He was about the first slave Marster had. He come from Virginny. They paid big money for him because he was a valuable darkey. He was about as valuable as the blacksmith.

[36]

I don't remember how much they paid for him, but it was big money.

Marster had sheep. In cold weather, women wore woolen dresses and coats; they called them jackets, and woolen stockings. And the men wore woolen socks and britches too. Everything they had was woven and made on the place. You didn't see any of them with a hat on them days. Our white folks didn't buy no hats for us. When we went to preaching, we had to go clean. I had a white pique bonnet with buttons. I thought bonnets looked mighty pretty when they done them up with flour starch. My wedding dress was made of white lawn with tucks and frills, long, pretty too. One of Mistis' nieces let me have her wedding veil, and I wore it. Fine, too!

A colored man named John Glauster married us. You know, he was just a man on the place what sung and prayed and he could give out the hymns. We belonged to the white folks' church, but we didn't go in at the door of the church though. They had a stairway on the outside where we could go up, and then after we got up the stairs we'd be in the church gallery. Mistis had a book. It was a catechism, and she asked us all the questions every Sunday. Marster let us have preaching in our cabins, too.

Poor white folks used to hang around the quarters, and if they could beat you out of anything they did. They'd trade the slaves out of their rations for calico and snuff. Some of the darkies sold their meat and meal, but if it was found out they got a good whipping.

The overseer on the plantation had a horn, a great big ram's horn. It was about two feet long. The overseer blowed it about two hours before day. The darkies had to get up and cook their breakfast and curry their mules and start for the field. They had better be in that field by sun-up. When the sun went down, they stuck their hoes up in the field and quit. Then they was free for the day.

Darkies had particular tasks to perform. Now, like if they was gath-

ering up corn, they shucked corn late to get it in the crib to keep it from being rained on. Sometimes, if they didn't get through before dark they held torches to see by.

Overseers didn't do no more than what Marster told him to. He'd come to the field and if he saw a slave sitting under a tree he'd ask him if he was sick, and it was all right if he was sick, but if he was well and laying out under a tree, he got a whipping. The overseer would go back and tell Marster, and that night he'd give them just as many licks as Marster said, but he was careful with the darkies. I never seed the overseer have a billie in his hand. His whip was wrapped around on the horn of his saddle. He'd unwrap it and put you on the clock and give you whatever Marster said. Overseers didn't have no rules, but if you resisted him, he'd double your whipping. For killing time or being lazy, you got twenty-five licks; for stealing, fifty licks; and for running away, that was the worst, if they got you back, you got a hundred licks. I had a cousin to run away, and they got her back from Charleston. The overseer give her a hundred licks. One lick cut the blood, and my Mistis got so mad she threwed that long hair back, I can see that long hair now, and quarreled at Marster. He said he had to make an example for the other slaves. Mistis said it injured the woman to whip her that way, so then Marster made them be more careful. Even that warn't as bad as going to the chain-gang now. Young darkies now gets mad with me for saying that, but they protected you, and nobody didn't need to bother you. They protected you wherever you went.

We had one man to run away to the North. He run away because the overseer whipped him because he went to the adjoining plantation to see a woman. You had to have a pass to go off the place, and he went without a pass. They never did hear nothing of him. They put the hounds on his trail but they never did catch him.

[38]

My mother was Marster's house girl. I just stayed around the house with Mistis. I was just, you might say, her little keeper. I stayed around, and waited on her, handed her water, fanned her, kept the flies off her, pulled up her pillow and done anything she'd tell me to do. My mother combed her hair and dressed her too.

Our Marsters kept patrollers to keep us straight. There was some hard-headed darkies like they is now who wanted to go without a pass, and if they didn't have a pass, the patrollers got them and brought them back home. There's a song about the patrollers. "Run, Nigger, run, the paddy-role will catch you, / Run, Nigger, run, the paddy-role will catch you, / Run, Nigger, run, the paddy-role will catch you. / You better get away, you better git away."

After some of the darkies was free they got bigoty and wanted to act so. The white folks put things over their faces and come round and scared us to death, but they never did do nothing to any of our Niggers. I was 'fraid they would. Mistis was afraid they might do something to my daddy, because he one of the uppity ones, so she had him to stay home at night, and they didn't get him. He was the carriage driver, and she was afraid for him.

When darkies got sick, they had herbs in the house. Senna was what they give you if you was bilious. It growed in the garden. Mistis had a bed of it. That's what she give you instead of salts. To keep off typhoid fever, if she could smell fever on you, she'd make a cup of purge grass, and that fever would break up. St. John leaves was good for chills and fever. White plantain tea was for weakly women. About the only things slaves needed to keep off diseases was good stout shoes on their feet, plenty to eat, good clothes, and when it started raining to quit work and come in. They had shelters in the fields for the men to go to if it started raining.

We had lots of fun on holidays. On New Year's Day we didn't work. Them Christmas Days was something else! If I could call back one of them Christmas Days now, when I went up to the house and brung back my checkered apron full! Lord, I was so happy! Great big round, peppermint balls! Big bunches of raisins, we put aprons full on the bed and then went back to the house to get another apron full.

We had good times at corn-shuckings too. Honey, I've seen my grandma, Icie, the cook, when they had corn-shuckings, the chickens she'd put in that big pot, hanging on one of them hooks in the kitchen fireplace. She put twelve chickens in that pot, grown hens, let them boil, put the dumplings in, call the darkies and give them a plate full. I just wish you could have been there and seen how my grandma made that gingerbread. They cooked that for corn-shuckings and used it for cake. It was better than what cake is now, and they give them locust beer to drink with it.

We had dances after the corn-shuckings. After they got through, the fiddler would start to fiddling and they would ring up in an old-time square dance. Everybody danced off to themselves. Just let your foot go backward and then let your foot go forward and whirl around. Men, too, danced that way, by themselves, and you could hear them darkies laugh! When we had cotton pickings, just like corn-shuckings, there was good things to eat and a dance afterwards. When we got through threshing, Marster give us a picnic. Marster didn't have to go off the place for nothing. He raised flour too. Then that was the time for our summer picnic. We'd have good things to eat, like at corn-shuckings, and Marster would give every one of the men a dram. Marster drawed it himself, had a big tin cup, and he'd take half a cupful for two men.

When Marster's chillun got married, we all seed the wedding. From the yard back down to what you call the first orchard, all the darkies

gathered. Every darkey from the quarters was there, men and women too. After it was through, all the darkies passed by the bride and groom and each one, men and women, said, "Oh! God bless you, Marster!" and squat. "Oh! God bless you, Mistis!" and squat. That's what we called dropping a courtsey. If the wedding was at a church, all the darkies come, and when the bride and groom come out and stood on the steps, all the darkies passed by and dropped a courtsey. It make them feel good for all the darkies to say that to them. The wedding dresses had trails as far as you could see. It took two folks to hold them up. My mother carried Young Mistis' trail, but of course after she carried the trail in the church, she went back to a place where you couldn't see, where the darkies was. Then when Young Mistis come out of the church, she picked up the trail and carried it again. All the time, when she would get in the carriage, her maid would hold up her trail for her.

Interviewed by Annie Lee Newton at Toccoa, July 15th, 1937.

WILLIS COFER

EDEN AND CALLINE COFER was my pa and ma and us all lived on the big Cofer plantation about five miles from Washington in Wilkes County. Pa belonged to Marse Henry Cofer and Ma and us chillun was the property of Marse Henry's father, Marse Joe Cofer.

Chilluns did have the best good times on our plantation, because Old Marster didn't allow them to do no work until they was twelve years old. Us just frolicked and played around the yard with the white chilluns, but us sure did evermore have to stay in that yard. It was the cook's place to boss us when the other Niggers was off in the fields, and every time us tried to slip off, she catched us and the way that woman would burn us up with a switch was a caution.

There warn't no schools for us to go to, so us just played around. Our cook was all time feeding us. Us had bread and milk for breakfast, dinner was mostly peas and cornbread, then supper was milk and bread. There was so many chilluns they fed us in a trough. They just poured the peas on the chunks of cornbread what they had crumbled in the trough, and us had to mussel them out. Yessum, I said mussel. The only spoon us had was mussel shells what us got out of the branches [streams]. A little Nigger could put peas and cornbread away mighty fast with a mussel shell.

Boys just wore shirts what looked like dresses till they was twelve years old and big enough to work in the field. Then they put them on pants made open in the back. All the boys was mighty proud when they got big enough to wear pants and to go to work in the fields with grown folks. When a boy got to be a man enough to wear pants, he drawed rations and quit eating out of the trough.

All the slave quarters was log cabins and little families had cabins with just one room. Old Marster sure did want to see lots of chilluns around the cabins and all the big families was allowed to live in two-room cabins. Beds for slaves was made by nailing frames, built out of oak or walnut planks to the sides of the cabins. They had two or three legs to make them set right, and the mattresses was filled with wheat straw. All our cooking was done in the fireplace. Pots was hung on iron cranes to boil and big pones of light bread was cooked in ovens on the hearth. That light bread and the biscuits made out of shortening was our Sunday bread, and they was sure good with our homemade butter. Us had old corn bread for our everyday bread.

There was four or five acres in Marster's big old garden, but then it took a big place to raise enough for all the slaves and white folkses, too, in the same garden. There was just the one garden with plenty of cabbage, collards, turnip greens, beans, corn, peas, onions, 'taters and just everything folks liked in the way of gardens. Marster never allowed but one smokehouse on his place. It was plumb full of meat, and every slave had his meat rations weighed out regular. There was just one dairy house too where the slaves got all the milk and butter they needed. Marster sure did believe in seeing that his Niggers had plenty to eat.

Marster raised lots of chickens and the slaves raised chickens too if they wanted to. Marster let them have land to work for themselves, but they had to work it after they come out of his fields. All they made on

this land was their own to sell and do what they wanted to with. Lots of them plowed and hoed by moonlight to make their own crops.

Us used to hear tell of big sales of slaves, when sometimes mammies would be sold away from their chilluns. It was awful. Then they would just cry and pray and beg to be allowed to stay together. Old Marster wouldn't do nothing like that to us. He said it warn't right for the chilluns to be took away from their mammies. At them sales they would put a Nigger on the scales and weigh him and then the bidding would start. If he was young and strong, the bidding would start around $150 and the highest bidder got the Nigger. A good young breeding woman brung $2,000 easy, because all the masters wanted to see plenty of strong healthy chillun coming on all the time. Carpenters and bricklayers and blacksmiths brung fancy prices from $3,000 to $5,000 sometimes. A Nigger what warn't no more than just a good field hand brung about $200.

Them bricklayers made all the bricks out of the red clay what they had right there on most of the plantations, and the blacksmith he had to make all the iron bars and cranes for the chimneys and fireplaces. He had to make the plow points, too, and keep the farm tools all fixed up. Sometimes at night they slipped off the place to go out and work for money, fixing chimneys and building things. But they better not let themselves get caught.

Mammy wove the cloth for our clothes and the white folkses had them made up. Quilts and all the bed-clothes was made out of homespun cloth.

The first Saturday after Easter was always a holiday for the slaves. Us was proud of that day because that was the onliest day in the year a Nigger could do exactly what he pleased. They could go hunting, fishing or visiting, but most of them used it to put in a good day's work on the land what Marster allowed them to use for themselves.

[44]

Us Niggers went to the white folks' churches. Mr. Louis Williams preached at the Baptist Church on the first Sundays and Methodist meetings was on the second Sundays. Mr. Andy Bowden and Mr. Scott Cowan was two of the Methodist preachers. Me and pa joined the Baptist Church. Ma was just a Methodist, but us all went to church together. They had the baptizing at the pool and there was sure a lot of praying and shouting and singing going on while the preacher done the dipping of them. The onliest one of them baptizing songs I can recollect now is, "Where the Healing Water Flows." They waited 'till they had a crowd ready to be baptized and then they took a whole Sunday for it and had a big dinner on the ground at the church.

The sure enough big days was them camp meeting days. White folks and Niggers all went to the same camp meeting, and they brung plenty along to eat—big old loafs of light bread what had been baked in the skillets. The night before they sat it in the ovens to rise and by morning it had done rise to the top of the deep old pans. They piled the red coals all around the ovens and when that bread got done it was good enough for anybody. The tables was loaded with barbecued pigs and lambs and all the fried chicken folks could eat, and all sorts of pies and cakes was spread out with the other goodies.

Every plantation generally had a barbecue and big dinner for Fourth of July, and when several white families went in together, they did have high old times trying to see which one of them could get their barbecue done and ready to eat first. They just ate and drunk all day. Us didn't know nothing about what they was celebrating on Fourth of July, except a big dinner and a good time.

When slaves got married, the man had to ask the gal's ma and pa for her and then he had to ask the white folks to allow them to get married. The white preacher married them. They hold right hands and the

preacher ask the man: "Do you take this gal to do the best you can for her?" And if he say yes, then they had to change hands and jump over the broomstick, and they was married. Our white folks was all church folks and didn't allow no dancing at weddings but they give them big suppers when their slaves got married. If you married some gal on another place, you just got to see her on Wednesday and Saturday nights and all the chilluns belonged to the gal's white folkses. You had to have a pass to go then, or the patrollers was sure to get you. Them patrollers evermore did beat up slaves if they caught them off their own master's place without no pass. If Niggers could out run them and get on their home lines they was safe.

On our place when a slave died they washed the corpse good with plenty of hot water and soap and wrapt it in a winding sheet, then laid it out on the cooling board and spread a snow white sheet over the whole business, till the coffin was made up. The winding sheet was sorter like a bed sheet made extra long. The cooling board was made like a ironing board except it had legs. White folkses was laid out that way same as Niggers. The coffins was made in a day. They took the measuring stick and measured the head, the body, and the footses and made the coffin to fit these measurements. If it was a man what died, they put a suit of clothes on him before they put him in the coffin. They buried the women in the winding sheets. When the Niggers got from the fields some of them went and dug a grave. Then they put the coffin on the ox-cart and carried it to the graveyard where they just had a burial that day. They waited about two months sometimes before they preached the funeral sermon. For the funeral they built a brush arbor in front of the white folks' church, and the white preacher preached the funeral sermon, and white folkses would come listen to slave funerals. The song most sung at funerals was "Hark from the Tomb." The reason they had

slave funerals so long after the burial was to have them on Sunday or some other time when the crops had been laid by so the other slaves could be on hand.

Our Marster done the overseeing at his place himself, and he never had no hired overseer. Nobody never got a licking on our plantation lessen they needed it bad, but when Marster did whip them they knowed they had been whipped. There warn't no fussing and fighting on our place and us all knowed better than to take what didn't belong to us, because Old Marster sure did get after Niggers what stole. If one Nigger did kill another Nigger, they took him and locked him in the jailhouse for thirty days to make his peace with God. Every day the preacher would come read the Bible to him, and when the thirty days was up, then they would hang him by the neck till he died. The man what done the hanging read the Bible to the folks what was gathered around there while the murderer was a-dying.

When us turned Marster's watch dogs loose at night, they warn't nothing could come around that place. They had to be kept chained up in the daytime. Sometimes Marster let us take his dogs and go hunting and they was the best 'possum trailers around them parts. When they barked up a persimmon tree, us always found a 'possum or two in that tree. Sometimes after us caught up lots of them, Marster let us have a 'possum supper. Baked with plenty of butter and 'tatoes and sprinkled over with red pepper, they is mighty good eatments.

After the war was over, they just turned the slaves loose without nothing. Some stayed on with Old Marster and worked for a little money and their rations. Ku Kluxers went around with them dough-faces on after the war. The Niggers got more beatings from them than they had ever got from their old masters. If a Nigger sassed white folkses or kilt a horse, them Kluxers sure did evermore beat him up. They

[47]

never touched me for I stayed out of their way, but they whupped my pa one time for being off his place after dark. When they turned him loose, he couldn't hardly stand up. The Yankees just about broke up the Ku Kluxers, but they sure was bad on Niggers while they lasted.

Pa went down on the Hubbard place and worked for forty dollars a year and his rations. Ma made cloth for all the folkses around about. They fetched their thread and she wove the cloth for fifty cents a day. If us made a good crop, us was all right with plenty of corn, peas, 'tatoes, cabbage, collards, turnip greens, all the hog meat us needed, and chickens, too. Us started out without nothing and had to go in debt to the white folkses at first but that was soon paid off. I never had no chance to go to school to get book learning. All the time us had to work in the fields.

Interviewed by Grace McCune at 548 Findley Street, Athens, in March, 1938.

MARTHA COLQUITT

WHEN I was born, my ma belonged to Marse Billie Glenn and us lived on his big plantation way down below Lexington. My pa was Anderson Mitchell. He come from Milledgeville and belonged to Mr. D. Smith. My ma was Healon Mitchell. I don't know what her last name was before she married. She was born in Virginny, and her and my grandma was sold and brought to Georgia when ma was a baby. Grandma never did see none of her other chillun or her husband no more, and us never did know nothing about them.

Ma had four chillun. Lucy was my only sister. Mr. Davenport bought her and she growed up at his place, which was called "The Glade." It was a big fine place at Point Peter, Georgia.

Ma's house was right on the edge of Marse Billie's yard, because she was the cook. Grandma lived in the same house with ma and us chillun, and she worked in the loom house and wove cloth all the time. She wove the checkidy cloth for the slaves' clothes and she made flannel cloth too. Leastways, it was part flannel. She made heaps of kinds of cloth.

Our beds had big home-made posts and frames, and us used ropes for springs. Grandma brought her feather bed with her from Virginny, and she used to piece up a heap of quilts out of our old clothes and any kind of scraps she could get hold of. I don't know what the others had in

their cabins because ma didn't allow her chillun to visit around the other folks none.

Ma's chillun all had victuals from the white folkses kitchen. After Marse Billie's family done ate and left the table, the cook was supposed to take what was left to feed the house Niggers and her own chillun, and us did have sure enough good victuals. All the other slave folks had their rations weighed out to them every week and they cooked in their own cabins. When the wheat was ground at the mill it made white flour and shorts and seconds. Most of the shorts was weighed out in rations for the slave folks. Now and then at Christmas and special times they got a little white flour. They liked cornbread for regular eating. They was always a lot of hogs on Marse Billie's plantation, and his colored folkses had plenty of side meat. Slaves never had no time to hunt in the day time, but they sure could catch lots of 'possums at night, and they knowed how to get catfish at night, too.

Cross the road from the Big House, Marse Billie had a big garden, and he seed that his help had plenty of something good to boil. They weren't no separate gardens. They didn't have no time to work no gardens of their own.

In summertime us chillun wore just one piece of clothes. It was a sack apron. In winter grandma made us yarn underskirts and yarn drawers buttoned down over our knees. Ma made our knit stockings. They called our brass-toed shoes brogans.

Marse Billie's overseer lived in a four-room house up the road a piece from the Big House. Nobody thought about none of Marse Billie's overseers as poor white folkses. Every overseer he ever had was decent and respectable. Course they weren't in the same class with Marse Billie's family, but they was all right. They was four or five homes nigh our plantation, but all of them belonged to rich white folkses. If they was

any poor white folkses around there, us chillun never heared nothing of them.

The overseer blowed a horn to wake them up just before day so as everybody could cook, eat and get out to the fields by sunrise. They quit nigh sundown, in time for them to feed the stock, do the milking, tend to bringing in the wood and all sorts of other little jobs that had to be done before it got too dark to see. They never was no work done at night on our plantation.

If any of Marse Billie's help was whipped, I never knowed nothing about it. They used to say that if any of them didn't work right the overseer would take them to the workshop. Us chillun never did know what happened when they took them to the workshop. It was too far away for us to hear what happened there. The workshop was a big lone shed off to itself, where they had the blacksmith place and where harnesses was mended and all sorts of fixing done to the tools and things.

On Christmas morning all of us would come up to the yard back of the Big House and Marse Billie and the overseer handed out presents for all. They was a little dram and cake, too. Us chillun got dolls and dresses and aprons. Them stuffed rag dolls was the prettiest things. On New Year's day all the men would come up to the Big House early in the morning and would work lively as they could a-cutting wood and doing all sorts of little jobs 'till the dinner bell rung. Then Marse Billie would come out and tell them they was starting the New Year right a-working lively and fast. Then he would say they be fed good and looked after good, long as they worked good. He give them a good taste of dram and cake all around, and let them go back to their cabins for dinner, and they could have the rest of the day to frolic.

Them cornshuckings us used to have sure was a sight. Corn would be piled up high as this house, and the folkses would dance around and

holler and whoop. Ma allowed us chillun to watch them about a half hour; then she made us come back inside our cabin because they always give the corn shucking folks some dram, and things would get lively and rough by the time all the corn was shucked.

When folks got sick, Marse Billie had them looked after. Mistress would come every day to see about them, and if she thought they was bad off, she sent after Dr. Davenport. Dr. Davenport come there so much 'till he courted and married Marse Billie's daughter, Miss Martha Glenn. I was named for Miss Martha. They sure did take special good care of the mammies and the babies. They had a separate house for them and a granny woman who didn't have nothing else to do but look after colored babies and mammies. The granny woman took the place of a doctor when the babies was born, but if she found a mammy in a bad fix she would ask Mistress to send for Dr. Davenport.

Us didn't have no separate church for colored folkses. The white folkses had a big Baptist church they called Mill Stone Church down at Goosepond, a good ways down the road from Marse Billie's plantation. It sure was a pretty sight to see, that church, all painted white and set in a big oak grove. Colored folkses had their place in the gallery. They weren't allowed to join the church on Sunday, but they had regular Saturday afternoons for the slaves to come and confess the faith and join the church. Us didn't know they was no other church but the Baptist. All the baptizing was done on Sunday by the white preacher. First he would baptize the white folkses in the pool back of the church, and then he would baptize the slaves in the same pool.

My grandma was a powerful Christian woman, and she did love to sing and shout. That's how come Marse Billie had her locked up the loom room when the Yankee men come to our plantation. Grandma would get to shouting so loud she would make so much fuss nobody in

the church could hear the preacher and she would wander off from the gallery and go downstairs and try to go down the white folks' aisles to get to the altar where the preacher was, and they was always locking her up for disturbing the worship. But they never could break her from that shouting and wandering around the meeting house even after she got old.

Them Yankee soldiers rode up in the Big House yard and begun to ask me questions about where Marse Billie was, and where everything on the place was kept, but I was too scared to say nothing. Everything was quiet and still as could be except for Grandma a-singing and a-shouting up in the loom house all by herself. One of them Yankees tried the door and he asked me how come it was locked up, and she told them the same thing I had told them. They asked her if she was hungry and she said she was. They took that axe and busted down the smoke-house door and told her she was free now and to help herself to any-thing she wanted, because everything on the plantation was to belong to the slaves that had worked there. They took grandma to the kitchen and told ma to give her some of the white folkses dinner. Ma said, "But the white folkses ain't ate yet." "Go right on," the Yankees said, "and give it to her, the best in the pot, and if they's anything left when she get through, maybe us will let the white folkses have some of it."

Them brash men strutted on through the kitchen into the house and they didn't see nobody else downstairs. Upstairs they didn't even have the manner to knock at Mistess' door. They just walked right on in where my sister, Lucy, was combing Mistess' long pretty hair. They told Lucy she was free now and not to do no more work for Mistess. Then all of them grabbed their big old rough hands into Mistess' hair, and they made her walk down stairs and out in the yard, and all the time they was a-pulling and jerking at her long hair, trying to make her

point out to them where Marse Billie had done had his horses and cattle hid out. Us chilluns was a-crying and taking on because us loved Mistess and us didn't want nobody to bother her. They made out like they was going to kill her if she didn't tell them what they wanted to know, but after awhile they let her alone.

After they had told all the slaves they could find on the place not to do no more work and to go help themselves to anything they wanted in the smokehouse and about the Big House and plantation, they rode on off, and us never seed no more of them. After the Yankees was done gone off Grandma begun to fuss, "Now, them soldiers was telling us what ain't so, because ain't nobody got no right to take what belongs to Marster and Mistress." And Ma joined in, "Sure it ain't no truth in what them Yankees was a-saying." And us went right on living just like us always done till Marse Billie called us together and told us the war was over and us was free to go where us wanted to go, and us could charge wages for our work.

When freedom come my pa wanted us to move off right away over to Mr. Smith's place so our family could be together, but us stayed on with Marse Billie the rest of that year. Then Pa and Ma moved to Lexington, where Pa digged wells and ditches and made right good pay. Ma took all four of us chillun and run a good farm. Us got along fine.

Interviewed by Sarah H. Hall at 190 Lyndon Avenue, Athens, in 1937.

BENNY DILLARD

M Y Mammy and Daddy, they warn't from this part of the country. My Mammy said that not long after she got to America from a trip on the water that took nigh six months to make, they brung her from Virginny and sold her down here in Georgia when she was just about sixteen years old. The onliest name she had when she got to Georgia was Nancy. I don't know where my Daddy come from. Him and Mammy was both sold to Marse Isaac Dillard and he took them to live on his place in Elbert County, close to the place they calls Goose Pond. They lived at home on that big old plantation. By that, I means that Marse Isaac growed everything needed to feed and clothe his folks except the little sugar, coffee and salt they used. I don't remember so much about times before the big war because I warn't but six years old when us was made free. Telling the slaves they was free didn't make much difference on our place, for most of them stayed right on there and worked with Old Marster just like they always done. That plantation was just like a little town—it was so big and it had everything us wanted and needed.

Slaves lived in log cabins what had red mud daubed in the cracks 'twixt the logs. The roofs was made out of boards what had so many cracks 'twixt them, after a few rains made them shrink, that us could lay

in bed and see the stars through them big holes. Even if us did have leaky houses, folks didn't get sick half as much as they does now. Our home-made beds was made out of rough planks nailed to high poles; leastways the poles was high for the headpieces, and a little lower for the footpieces. For most of them beds, planks was nailed to the wall for one long side and there was two legs to make it stand straight on the other long side. They never seed no metal springs them days but just wove cords back and forth, up and down and across, to lay the mattress on. I never seed no sto'-bought bed 'till after I was married. Bedticks was made out of homespun cloth stuffed with wheatstraw, and sometimes they slept on rye or oatstraw. Pillows was stuffed with hay what had a little cotton mixed in it sometimes. After a long day of work in the fields, nobody bothered about what was inside them pillows. They slept mighty good like they was. They fixed planks to slide across the inside of the holes they cut out for windows. The doors swung on pegs what took the place of the iron hinges they uses these days. Them old stack chimneys was made out of sticks and red mud.

The fireplaces was a heap bigger than they has now, for all the cooking was done in open fireplaces then. 'Taters and cornpone was roasted in the ashes and most of the other victuals was boiled in the big old pots what swung on cranes over the coals. They had long-handled frying pans and heavy iron skillets with big, thick, tight-fitting lids and ovens of all sizes to bake in. All of them things was used right there in the fireplace. There never was no better tasting something to eat than that cooked in them old cook-things in open fireplaces.

Chillun never had no work to do. They just ate and frolicked around gitting into everything they could find. They never got no lickings unless they was mighty bad, because our Marster said he warn't going to allow no beating on his Niggers except what he done his own self, and

[56]

that was powerful little. In hot weather chillun played in the creek and the best game of all was to play like it was big meeting time. White chillun loved to play there, too, with the little slave chillun. Us would have make-believe preaching and baptizing and the way us would sing was a sight. One day our Marster hid in the trees and watched us because Mistess had done been fussing down about chillun all coming in soaked to the hide. He waited 'till he seed all the preaching and baptizing, then he hollered for us to stop and he took the ones what was doing all the baptizing and made them pray and sing; then he ducked them good in the water and made us all go up to the house to show Mistess how come so many of them poor chillun had done been getting wet so much. Us got a tanning then that Marster allowed would help us to get sure enough religion.

The wooden bowls what slave chillun ate out of was made out of sweetgum trees. Us ate with mussel shells instead of spoons. Them mussel shells was all right. Us could use them to get up plenty of bread and milk, or cornpone soaked with peas and pot liquor. They never let chillun have no meat 'till they was big enough to work in the fields. Us had biscuit once a week; that was Sunday breakfast, and them biscuits was cakebread to us. The first bought meat us chillun ever seed was a slab of side-meat Daddy got from the store after us had done left the plantation, and us was scared to eat it because it warn't like what us had been used to.

Chillun just wore one piece of clothes in summertime and they all went barefoots. The gals' summer garment was a plain, sleeveless apron dress, and the boys wore skimpy little shirts and nothing else. They mixed cow-hair with the cotton when they wove the cloth to make our winter clothes out of. That cow-hair cloth sure could scratch, but it was good and warm and Marster seed to it that us had all the clothes us

needed. The womans made all the cloth used on the place; they carded, spun and then wove it. Mammy was the weaver; that was all she done, just wove cloth. They dyed it with red mud and ink balls and such like.

Marster never liked to get up real early himself in slavery time, so he had one man what got the Niggers up out of bed so early that they had done ate breakfast and was in the field when daylight come. After the war was over and everybody was free, all the Niggers used to just piddle and play around every morning whilst they was waiting for Marster to come. Them and the mules would be just a-standing still and when the word was passed that Marster had done got up all of them would start off with a rush, just a-hollering: "Whoa, dar! Gee haw!" just like they had done been working hard all morning. One day Marster catched them at it, and he didn't say a word 'till time come to pay off, and he took out for all the time they had lost.

Sometimes slaves run away and hid out in caves. They would pile up rocks and sticks and pine limbs to hide the caves, and sometimes they would stay hid out for weeks, and the other Niggers would slip them something to eat at night. There warn't many what run off on our place, because our Marster was so good to all of them that there warn't nothing to run from.

Marster made all his work tools at home. Plowsheers was made out of wood trimmed to the right shape and fastened to an iron point. When they was plowing in the young cotton, they nailed a board on one side of the plow to rake the dirt back up around the cotton plants.

Marster's gin was turned by a mule. That big old gin wheel had wooden cogs what made the gin work when the old mule went around and around hitched to that wheel. That old cotton press was a sight. First they cut down a big old tree and trimmed off the limbs and made grooves in it for planks to fit in. It was stood up with a big weight on top

of it, over the cotton what was to be pressed. It was worked by a wheel what was turned by a mule, just like the one what turned the gin. An old mule pulled the pole what turned the syrup mill, too. Them old mules done their part along side the Niggers them days, and Marster seed that his mules had good care too. When them mules had done turned the mill 'till the juice was squeezed out of the sugar cane stalks, they strained that juice and boiled it down 'till it was just the finest tasting syrup you ever did see. Marster's mill where he ground his wheat and corn was down on the crick, so the water could turn the big old wheel.

Them old cornshuckings was sure enough big times, because us raised so much corn that it took several days to shuck it all. Us had to have two generals. They chose sides and then they got up on top of the biggest piles of corn and kept the slaves a-singing fast so they would work fast. The first crowd what finished got the prize. There ain't much I can remember of words to them old cornshucking songs. One general would start off singing: "Shuck up this corn, / shuck up this corn, / 'cause us is going home," and the other general would be a-shouting: "Make them shucks fly, make them shucks fly, us is going to go home." Over and over they kept on singing them lines. Come nighttime Marster would have big bonfires built up and set out torches for them to see how to work, and every time he passed around that jug of corn liquor shucks would fly faster. When all the corn was done shucked and the big supper had been ate, there was wrestling matches and dancing and all sorts of frolicking.

During of the war time, soda and salt was both hard to get. They boiled down the dirt from under old smokehouses to get salt, and soda was made out of burnt corncobs. You would be surprised to see what good cooking could be done with that old corncob soda.

[59]

Us worked for Mr. Green Hubbard the first year us left the old plantation, but he wouldn't pay us so us left him and rented some land to farm. Then I went to work for Mr. Stephens and stayed with him twenty-five years.

Interviewed by Grace McCune at Athens, in 1938.

CALLIE ELDER

I WAS BORN in Floyd County, up nigh Rome, Georgia, on Marse Billy Neal's plantation. Ann and Washington Neal was my Mammy and Pappy. No preacher never married them. Marse Billy Neal, he owned both of them and after my Pappy asked him could he marry Mammy, Marse Billy made them go up to the hall of the big house and jump backwards over a broom.

There was six of us chillun—me and Frances, Beulah, Thomas, Felix and Scott. There was mighty little work done by chillun in slavery days. I just played around and kicked up my heels with the rest of the chillun.

Our log cabins what us lived in was daubed inside and out with mud to keep out bad weather. Our beds was held together by cords what was twisted every which way. You had to be mighty careful tightening them cords or the beds was liable to fall down. Us slept on wheat straw mattresses and had plenty of good warm quilts for cover.

Grown folks was fed cornbread and meat with plenty of vegetables in the week days and on Sunday mornings they give them wheat bread, what was something slaves didn't see no more 'till the next Sunday morning. About four o'clock on summer afternoons, they set a big old wooden bowl full of cornbread crumbs out in the yard and poured in

buttermilk or potliquor 'till the crumbs was covered. Then they let the chillun gather around it and eat 'till de bowl was empty. In winter chillun was fed inside de house.

Our clothes was made new for us in the fall out of cloth wove in looms right thar on the plantation. Top clothes was dyed with hickory bark. The full skirts was gathered to tight fitting waists. Underskirts was made the same way. The dresses had done wore thin enough for hot weather by the time winter was gone so us wore them same clothes straight on through the summer, only us left off the underskirts then. Slave chillun didn't never wear no shoes. Our foots cracked open 'till they looked like goose foots. Us wore the same on Sunday as every day, except that our clothes was clean and stiff with meal starch when us got into them on Sunday mornings.

Marse Billie Neal was our owner and Miss Peggy was his old woman. They was just as good to us as they could be. Their two chillun was Marse Tom and Marse Mid. The carriage driver never had much to do but drive Marse Billy and Miss Peggy around and, of course he had to see that the horses and carriage was kept clean and shiny. I don't remember if he took the chillun around.

I sure can't tell nothing at all about how big that old plantation was, but it was one whopping big place. There was too many slaves on that plantation for me to count. The overseer got them up by four o'clock and the men had to be in the fields by sunrise. The womans went out about eight o'clock. They stopped work at sundown and by the time they ate and done the chores for the day it was ten o'clock before they hit the bed. The cabins was built in a circle and the overseer went the rounds every night to see if the slaves was in bed.

Yes Ma'am, they whipped the Niggers. My Pappy and Grandpa was the worst ones about gitting licked. Every time Pappy runned away

Marse Billy sicked them hounds on his heels and they was sure to catch him and fetch him back. They had to keep knives from Pappy or when them dogs catched him he would just cut them up so they would die. When they got him back to the house, they would buckle him down over a barrel and larrup him with a plaited whip. Womans warn't whipped much. My grandpa York was so bad about running away Marse Billy made him wear long old horns. One Sunday Marse Billy went by our church to see if all his Niggers was thar what was supposed to be thar. And there grandpa was a-sitting with them horns on his head. Marse Billy told him he could take the horns off his head whilst he was in the meeting house. At that grandpa dropped them horns and lit a rag to the woods and it took the dogs days to find him. None of our Niggers ever runned away to the North. They was too busy running off to the woods. Just to tell the truth them Niggers on our place was so dumb they didn't even take in about no North. They didn't even know what the war was about 'till it was all over.

If one slave killed another, Marse Billy made the overseer tie that dead Nigger to the one what killed him, and the killer had to drag the corpse around till he died, too. The murderers never lived long a-dragging them dead ones around. There was a guard house on the farm, where the worst Niggers was kept, and while they was in that guard house, they warn't fed but once a day. It warn't nothing unusual for Marse Billy to sell slaves, but he never sold his best Niggers. The ones he sold was always them he couldn't get no work out of.

Not a Nigger could read or write on Marse Billy's plantation. There was a shackly sort of church house on our plantation and on Sundays after the Niggers had cleaned theirselves up, if they told Marse Billy they wanted to go to church, he sent them on. All I knows about baptizings is they just took them to the river and plunged them in. They

sung someping about: "Going to the River for to be Baptized." Us had prayer meetings on Wednesday nights sometimes.

Don't ax me about funerals. I got the misery in my legs, and I feels too bad this morning to let myself even think about funerals. Back then when slave folks died they just put them in home-made pine coffins what they throwed in a wagon and took them to the graveyard. At them buryings, they used to sing: "Am I born to die / To let this body down."

What the slaves done on Saturday night? They done anything they was big enough to do. There warn't no frolicking except on Saturday night. Niggers on our place worked all day Saturday except once a month. Some of the slaves would slip off and stay half a day and the overseer wouldn't miss them because there was so many in the field. It was just too bad for any Nigger what got catched at that trick. Saturday night, slaves was allowed to git together and frolic and cut the buck.

Christmas Day Marse Billy called us to the big house and give us a little fresh meat and sweet bread that was cake. Christmas warn't much different from other times. Just more to eat. Us just had that one day off, and New Year's Day was used as a holiday, too.

Oh, them cornshuckings! All day before a cornshucking they hauled corn and put it in great piles as high as this here house. Us sung all the time us was shucking corn. There was a lot of them old shucking songs. The one us sung most was: "Whooper John and Calline all night." Marse Billy, he give them coffee and whiskey all night and that made them get rough and rowdy. Then the shucks did fly. Us had one more grand feast when the last ear of corn had done been shucked. There warn't nothing lacking.

Cotton pickings warn't planned for fun and frolic like cornshuckings. If Marse Billy got behind in his crops, he just sent us back to the fields at night when the moon was bright and sometimes us picked cotton all

night long. Marster give the woman what picked the most cotton a day off, and the man what picked the most had the same privilege.

Old Aunt Martha what nursed the chillun while their Mammies worked in the field was the quilting manager. It warn't nothing for womans to quilt three quilts in one night. Them quilts had to be finished before they stopped to eat a bit of the quilting feast. Marse Billy divided them quilts out amongst the Niggers what needed them most.

Our white folks was good as they knowed how to be when us got sick. I don't 'member that they ever had a doctor for the slaves, but they give us all kinds of home-brewed teas. Pinetops, mullein and fat lightwood splinters was biled together and the tea was our cure for different ailments. Scurvy grass tea mixed with honey was good for stomach troubles, but you sure couldn't take much of it at a time. It was the movingest medicine! Around our necks us wore asafetida sacks tied on strings soaked in turpentine. That was to keep diseases off of us.

What does I remember about de war? Well, it was fit to fetch our freedom. Marse Billy had a fine stallion. When the soldiers was coming, he sent Pappy to the woods with that stallion and some gold and told him not to let them Yankees find them. That stallion kept squealing 'till the Yankees found him, and they took him and the gold, too. Grandma was a-churning away out on the back porch and she had a ten dollar gold piece what she didn't want them soldiers to steal, so she drapped it in the churn. Them Yankees poured that buttermilk out right thar on the porch floor and got grandma's money. Marse Billy hid himself in a den with some more money and other things and they didn't find him. They took what they wanted of what they found and give the rest to the slaves. After the soldiers left, the Niggers give it all back to Marster because he had always been so good to them.

Us stayed on with Marse Billy for several years after the war. He

paid us $10 a month and he allowanced out the rations to us every week; most always on Monday because Sundays us had enough company to eat it all at one time. He give us three pounds of fat meat, a peck of meal, a peck of flour, 25¢ worth of sugar and a pound of coffee. That had to last a whole week.

Interviewed by Sadie B. Hornsby at 640 West Hancock Avenue, Athens.

ELISHA GAREY

I WAS BORN on the upper edge of Hart County, near Shoal Creek. Sarah Anne Garey was my Ma, and I was one of them shady babies. There was plenty of that kind in them times. My own sister was Rachel, and I had a half sister named Sallie what was white as anybody. John, Lindsay, David, and Joseph was my four brothers.

What did us chillun do? Us worked like horses. Didn't nobody eat there unless they worked. I'se been working ever since I come in this world.

Us lived in log huts. Every hut had a entry in the middle and a mud chimney at each end. Us slept in beds what was attached to the side of the hut, and they was boxed up like wagon bodies to hold the corn shucks and the babies in. Home-made rugs was put on top of the shucks for sheets, and the cover was the same thing.

I still remembers my grandma Rachel. The traders fetched her here from Virginia, and she never did learn to talk plain. Grandma Sallie Gaines was too old for field work, so she looked after the slave babies whilst their ma's was working in the field. Grandpa Jack Gaines was the shoemaker.

Most of the time I was up at the big house waiting on our white folks, hunting eggs, picking up chips, making fires and little jobs like that.

[67]

The onliest way I could find to make any money in them days was to sell partridges what I catched in traps to them Yankees what was always passing around. They paid me ten cents apiece for partridges and I might have saved more of my money if I hadn't loved that store-bought peppermint candy so good.

What I ate? Anything I could get. Peas, green corn, potatoes, corn-bread, meat and lye hominy was what they give us more than anything else. Baking was done in big old ovens what held three pones of bread and in skillets what held two. Big pots for boiling was swung over the coals in the fireplace. They was hung on hooks fastened to the chimney or on cranes what could be swung off fire when they wanted to dish up the victuals. It warn't nothing for us to catch five or six 'possums in one night's hunting. The best way to tote 'possums is to split a stick and run their tails through the crack, then fling the stick across your shoulders and tote the 'possums along safe and sound. That way they can't bite you. They's bad about gnawing out of sacks. When us went gigging at night, us most always fetched back a heap of fishes and frogs. There was always plenty of fish and rabbits. Our good old hound dog was just about as good at trailing rabbits in the daytime as he was at treeing 'possums at night. I was young and spry, and it didn't seem to make no difference what I ate them days. Big gardens was scattered over the place wherever Marster happened to pick out a good garden spot. Them gardens all belonged to our Marster, but he fed us all us wanted out of them.

All that us chillun wore in summer was just one little shirt. It was a long time before us knowed there was folks anywhere that put more than one piece of clothes on chillun in summer. Grandpa Jack made the red shoes us wore without no socks in winter. Our other winter clothes was cotton shirts and pants and coats what had a little wool in them.

Summer times us went bare-headed, but Uncle Ned made bullrush hats for us to wear in winter. There weren't no different clothes for Sunday. We toted our shoes along in our hands going to church. Us put them on just before us got there and took them off again soon as us got out of sight of the meeting house on the way back home.

Marse Joe Glover was a good man and he never whipped his Niggers much. His wife, our Miss Julia, was all right too—that she was. Their three chilluns was Miss Sue, Miss Puss and Marster Will. Marse Joe done all his own overseeing. He used to tuck his long white beard inside his shirt and button it up.

That was a fine looking turn-out of Marse Joe's—that rock-a-way carriage with bead fringe all around the canopy, a pair of spanking black horses hitched to it, and my brother, David, setting so proud like up on the high seat they put on the top for the driver.

There warn't no slave, man or woman, living on that plantation what knowed how many acres was in it. I expect there was as many as 500 slaves in all. Marster appointed a colored boy to get the slaves up before day, and they worked from sunup to sundown.

Jails? There was several little houses that held about two or three folks what they called jails. White folks used to get locked up in them but I never did see no Niggers in one of them little jailhouses. I never seen no Niggers sold, but I did see them in wagons going to Mississippi to be sold. I never seen no slave in chains.

Some few slaves could read and write, and them what could read was most always called on by the others for preaching. Charlie McCollie was the first colored preacher I ever seen. White folks allowed slaves to make brush arbors for churches on the plantations, and Nigger boys and gals done some tall courting at them brush arbors. That was the onliest place where you could get to see the gals you liked the best. They

used to start off services singing, "Come Ye that Loves the Lord." Warn't no pools in the churches to baptize folks in them, so they took them down to the creek. First a deacon went in and measured the water with a stick to find a safe and suitable place. Then they was ready for the preacher and the candidates. Everybody else stood on the banks of the creek and joined in the singing. Some of them songs was: "Lead Me to the Water for to be Baptized," "Oh, How I love Jesus" and "Oh, Happy Day that Fixed my Choice."

How in the name of the Lawd could slaves run away to the North with them Nigger dogs on their heels? I never knowed nary one to run away. Patrollers never runned me none, but they did get after some of the other slaves a whole lot. Marse Joe always had one pet slave what he sent news by.

When slaves come in from the fields at night, they was glad to just go to bed and rest their bones. They stopped off from field work at dinner time Saturdays. Saturday nights us had stomp down good times picking the banjo, blowing on quills, drinking liquor and dancing. I was sure one fast Nigger then. Sunday was meeting day for grown folks and gals. Boys throwded rocks and hunted birds' nests that day.

Christmas morning us chillun was up before squirrels, looking up the chimney for Santa Claus. There was plenty to eat then—syrup, cake, and everything.

New Year's Day the slaves all went back to work with most of them clearing new ground that day. There was always plenty to do. The only other holidays us had was when us was rained out or if sleet and snow drove us out of the fields. Everybody had a good time then a-frolicking. When us was tracking rabbits in the snow, it was heaps of fun.

Marse Joe had piles and piles of corn lined up in a ring for the corn shuckings. The general pitched the songs and the Niggers would follow,

keeping time a-singing and shucking corn. After all the corn was shucked, they gave a big feast with lots of whiskey to drink and the slaves was allowed to dance and frolic 'till morning.

If a neighbor got behind in gathering his cotton, Marse Joe sent his slaves to help pick it out by moonlight. Times like them days, us ain't never going to see no more.

I ain't never seen no such time in my life as they had when Marse Will Glover married Miss Moorehead. She had on a white satin dress with a veil over her face, and I declare to goodness I never seen such a pretty white lady. Next day after the wedding day, Marse Will had the affair at his house and I knows I ain't never been where so much good to eat was set out in one place as they had that day. I ate so much I was scared I warn't going to be able to go along back to Marse Joe's plantation with the rest of them.

Old Marster put every foot forward to take care of his slaves when they took sick, because they was his own property. They poured assafetida and pine top tea down us and made us take tea of some sort or another for almost all of the ailments there was them days. Slaves wore a nickel or a copper on strings around their necks to keep off sickness. Some few of them wore a dime; but dimes was hard to get.

One game us chillun played was "doodle." Us would find us a doodle hole and start calling the doodle bug to come out. You might talk and talk but if you didn't promise him a jug of molasses he wouldn't come up to save your life. One of the songs us sung playing chillun's games was sorter like this: "Whose been here / Since I been gone? / A pretty little gal / With a blue dress on."

Joy was on the way when us heard about freedom, if us did have to whisper. Marse Joe had done been killed in the war by a bomb. Mistress, she just cried and cried. She didn't want us to leave her, so us

stayed on with her a long time; then us went off to Mississippi to work on the railroad.

Interviewed by Sadie B. Hornsby at 258 Lyndon Avenue, Athens.

LEAH GARRETT

I KNOW so many things about slavery time 'till I never will be able to tell them all. In them days, preachers was just as bad and mean as anybody else. There was a man who folks called a good preacher, but he was one of the meanest men I ever seen. When I was in slavery under him he done so many bad things 'till God soon killed him. His wife or chillun could git mad with you, and if they told him anything he always beat you. Most times he beat his slaves when they hadn't done nothing at all. One Sunday morning his wife told him their cook wouldn't never fix nothing she told her to fix. Time she said it he jumped up from the table, went in the kitchen and made the cook go under the porch where he always whipped his slaves. She begged and prayed but he didn't pay no attention to that. He put her up in what us called the swing, and beat her 'till she couldn't holler. The poor thing already had heart trouble; that's why he put her in the kitchen, but he left her swinging there and went to church, preached and called himself serving God. When he got back home she was dead. Whenever your master had you swinging up, nobody wouldn't take you down. Sometimes a man would help his wife, but most times he was beat afterwards.

Another master I had kept a hogshead to whip you on. The hogshead had two or three hoops around it. He buckled you face down on

the hogshead and whipped you 'till you bled. Everybody always stripped you in them days to whip you, because they didn't care who seed you naked. Some folks' chillun took sticks and jabbed you all while you was being beat. Sometimes these chillun would beat you all across your head, and their Ma's and Pa's didn't know what stop was.

Another way Marster had to whip us was in a stock that he had in the stables. This was where he whipped you when he was real mad. He had logs fixed together with holes for your feet, hands and head. He had a way to open these logs and fasten you in. Then he had his coachman give you so many lashes, and he would let you stay in the stock for so many days and nights. That's why he had it in the stable so it wouldn't rain on you. Everyday you got that same number of lashes. You never come out able to sit down.

I had a cousin with two chillun. The oldest one had to nurse one of Marster's grandchildren. The front steps was real high, and one day this poor child fell down these steps with the baby. His wife and daughter hollered and went on terrible, and when our master come home they was still hollering just like the baby was dead or dying. When they told him about it, he picked up a board and hit this poor little child across the head and killed her right there. Then he told his slaves to take her and throw her in the river. Her Ma begged and prayed, but he didn't pay her no attention; he made them throw the child in.

One of the slaves married a young gal, and they put her in the Big House to work. One day Mistess jumped on her about something and the gal hit her back. Mistess said she was going to have master put her in the stock and beat her when he come home. When the gal went to the field and told her husband about it, he told her where to go and stay 'till he got there. That night he took his supper to her. He carried her to a cave and hauled pine straw and put in there for her to sleep on. He

[74]

fixed that cave up just like a house for her, put a stove in there and run the pipe out through the ground into a swamp. Everybody always wondered how he fixed that pipe. Of course, they didn't cook on it until night when nobody could see the smoke. He sealed the house with pine logs, made beds and tables out of pine poles, and they lived in this cave seven years. During this time, they had three chillun. Nobody was with her when these chillun was born but her husband. He waited on her with each child. The chillun didn't wear no clothes except a piece tied round their waists. They was just as hairy as wild people, and they was wild. When they come out of that cave they would run every time they seed a person.

The seven years she lived in the cave, different folks helped keep them in food. Her husband would take it to a certain place, and she would go and get it. People had passed over this cave ever so many times, but nobody knowed these folks was living there. Our Marster didn't know where she was, and it was freedom before she come out of that cave for good.

Us lived in a long house that had a flat top and little rooms made like mule stalls, just big enough for you to git in and sleep. They warn't no floors in these rooms and neither no beds. Us made beds out of dry grass, but us had cover because the real old people, who couldn't do nothing else, made plenty of it. Nobody warn't allowed to have fires, and if they was caught with any that meant a beating. Some would burn charcoal and take the coals to their rooms to help warm them. Every person had a tin pan, a tin cup and a spoon. Everybody couldn't eat at one time; us had about four different sets. Nobody had a stove to cook on; everybody cooked on fire places and used skillets and pots. To boil us hung pots on racks over the fire and baked bread and meats in the skillets.

[75]

Marster had a big room right side his house where victuals was cooked. Then the cook had to carry them upstairs in a tray to be served. When the something to eat was carried to the dining room it was put on a table and served from this table. The food warn't put on the eating table.

The slaves went to church with their masters. The preachers always preached to the white folks first; then they would preach to the slaves. They never said nothing but you must be good, don't steal, don't talk back to your masters, don't run away, don't do this and don't do that. They let colored preachers preach but they give them almanacs to preach out of. They didn't allow us to sing such songs as "We Shall Be Free" and "O For a Thousand Tongues to Sing." They always had somebody to follow the slaves to church when the colored preacher was preaching to hear what was said and done. They was afraid us would try to say something against them.

Interviewed by Louise Oliphant in Augusta.

CHARLIE HUDSON

I WAS BORN March 27, 1858 in Elbert County. Ma lived on the Bell plantation and Marse Matt Hudson owned my Pa and kept him on the Hudson place. There was seven of us chillun. Will, Bynam, John and me was the boys, and the gals was Amanda, Liza Ann and Gussie. 'Till us was big enough to work, us played around the house about like chillun does these days.

Slave quarters was laid out like streets. Us lived in log cabins. Beds? They was just makeshift beds, what was made out of pine poles. The side of the house was the head of the beds. The side rails was sharpened at both ends and drive in holes in the walls and foot posts. Then they put boards across the side rails for the mattresses to lay on. The coarse cloth bed ticks was filled with "Georgy feathers." Don't you know what Georgy feathers was? Wheat straw was Georgy feathers. Our cover was sheets and plenty of good warm quilts. Now that was at our own quarters on Marse David Bell's plantation.

Didn't everybody have as good places to sleep as us. I remembers a white family named Sims what lived in Flatwoods. They was the poorest white folks I ever seed. They had a big drove of chillun and their Pa never worked a lick in his life. He just lived on other folks' labors. Their little log cabin had a partition in it, and behind that partition

there warn't a stitch of nothing. They didn't have no floor but the ground, and back behind that partition was dug out a little deeper than in the rest of the house. They filled that place with leaves and that's where all the chilluns slept. Every day Miss Sallie made them take out the leaves what they had slept on the night before and fill the dugout with fresh leaves. On the other side of the partition, Miss Sallie and her old man slept along with their hog and horse and cow and that was where they cooked and ate, too. I ain't never going to forget them white folks.

My grandma Patsy, Pappy's Ma, knocked around looking after the sheep and hogs, close to the house, because she was too old for field work. Ma's Mammy was my grandma Rose. Her job was driving the oxcart to haul in wood from the new grounds and to take wheat and corn to mill and fetch back good old home-made flour and meal. I never did hear nothing about my grandpas. Ma done the cooking for the white folks.

I don't know if I was no pet, but I did stay up at the big house most of the time, and one thing I loved to do up there was to follow Miss Betsy around toting her sewing basket. When work got tight and hot in crop time, I helped the other chillun tote water to the hands. The bucket would slamp against my legs all along the way, and most of the water would be done splashed out before I got to the field.

Marse David and his family most always sent their notes and messages by me and another yearling boy what was allowed to lay around the big house yard so us would be handy to wait on our white folks. They give you the note what they done writ, and they say: "Boy, if you lose this note, you'll get a whupping." All the time you was carrying them notes you had your whupping in your hand and didn't know it, lessen you lost the note. I never heard of no trouble to amount to nothing twixt white folks and Niggers in our settlement.

Us ate good, not much different from what us does now. Most times it was meat and bread with turnip greens, hominy, milk and butter. All our cooking was done on open fireplaces. Oh! I was fond of 'possums, sprinkled with butter and pepper and baked down 'till de gravy was good and brown. You was lucky if you got to eat 'possum and gnaw the bones after my Ma done cooked it.

They catched rabbits with dogs. Now and then, a crowd of Niggers would jump a rabbit when no dogs was around. They would throw rocks at him and run him in a hollow log. Then they would twist him out with hickory wisps. Sometimes there warn't no fur left on the rabbit time they got him twisted out, but that was all right. They just slapped him over dead and took him on to the cabin to be cooked. Rabbits was most generally fried.

Grown boys didn't want us chillun going along 'possum hunting with them, so all right, they took us way off crost the fields 'till they found a good thick clump of bushes, and then they would holler out that there was some mighty fine snipes around there. They made us hold de poke [bag] open so the snipes could run in. Then they blowed out their lightwood knot torches and left us chillun holding the poke whilst they went on hunting 'possums.

After dinner Saturdays all of us took our hooks, poles and lines down to Dry Fork Creek, when it was the right time of the year to fish. Sometimes they stewed fish for old folks to eat, but young folks loved them fried best.

Winter time they give chillun new cotton and wool mixed shirts what come down most to the ankles. By the time hot weather come the shirt was done wore thin and shrunk up and besides that, us had growed enough for them to be short on us, so us just wore them same shirts right on through the summer. On our place you went bare foots 'till you was

[79]

a great big yearling before you got no shoes. What you wore on your head was a cap made out of scraps of cloth they wove in the looms right thar on our plantation to make pants for the grown folks.

Mr. David Bell, our Marster, was born clubfooted. His hands and foots was drawn up every which a way long as he lived. He was just like a old tom cat, he was such a cusser. All he done was just set there and cuss, and a heap of times you couldn't see nothing for him to cuss about. He took his crook-handled walking stick and catched you and drug you up to him and then just held you tight and cussed you to your face, but he didn't never whip nobody. Our Mistess, Miss Betsey, was always mighty kind at times like that, and she used to give us chillun a heap of ginger cakes. Their seven chilluns was Dr. Bynam, Marse David and little Misses Adeline, Elizabeth, Mary and Mildred. They lived in a big old two-story house.

That overseer, he was a clever man, but I can't recollect his name. He never paid no heed to what sort of clothes slaves wore, but he used to raise merry cain if they didn't have good shoes to ditch in. Marse David was the cussing boss, but de overseer called himself the whupping boss. He had whuppings all time saved up special for the womans. He made them take off their waists and then he whipped them on their bare backs till he was satisfied. He done all the whupping after supper by candle light. I don't remember that he ever whipped a man. He just whipped womans.

Everybody was up early so that by sunrise they was out in the fields, just a whooping and hollering. At sundown they stopped and come back to the cabins. In wheat harvesting time they worked so hard they just fell out from gitting overheated. Other times they just worked along steady like.

Marse David never had no sure enough carriage so he never needed

no carriage driver. He had what they called a ground sleigh. In the spring Marse David sent a man to the woods to pick out a likely looking young white oak sapling and bent it down a certain way. It stayed bent that way 'till it growed big enough, then they sawed it lengthways and put a mortise hole in each front piece to put the round through to hold the singletrees. Holes was bored at the back to fasten the plank seat to. They put a quilt on the seat for a cushion and hitched a pair of oxen to the sleigh. Come winter, come summer, snow or rain, they went right on in the old sleigh just the same!

They didn't have no jail house or nothing like that around that plantation, because if slaves didn't please Marster they was just made to come up to the yard at the big house and take their beatings. I seed them traders come through from Virginny with two wagon loads of slaves at one time, going down on Broad River to a place called Lisbon where they already had orders for them. I ain't never seed no slaves being sold or auctioned off on the block.

Once a white man named Bill Rowsey come and begged Marse David to let him teach his Niggers. Marse David had the grown mens go sweep up the cottonseed in the ginhouse on Sunday morning, and for three Sundays us went to school. When us went on the fourth Sunday night riders had done made a shape like a coffin in the sand out in front and painted a sign on the ginhouse what read: "No Niggers allowed to be taught in this ginhouse." That made Marse David so mad he just cussed and cussed. He allowed that nobody warn't going tell him what to do. But us was too scared to go back to the ginhouse to school. Next week Marse David had them build a brush arbor down by the crick, but when us went down thar on Sunday for school, us found the night riders had done destroyed the brush arbor, and that was the end of my going to school.

[81]

There warn't no church for slaves where us was. Marse David give us a pass so us wouldn't be disturbed and let us go around from one plantation to another on Sundays for prayer meetings in the cabins and under trees if the weather was warm and nice. Sometimes when there was a jubilee coming off, slaves was allowed to go to their Marster's church. Me? I used to ride behind Miss Betsey on her horse what she called Puss and away us went jigging down the road to jubilees at Millstone and Elam churches. I was a rich feeling little Nigger then.

The chillun had to take a back seat whilst the old folks done all the singing, so I never learned none of them songs good enough to remember what the words was or the tunes neither. Now and then us went to a funeral, not often, but if there was a baptizing inside of ten miles around from where us lived, us didn't miss it. Us knowed how to walk and went to git the pleasure.

After slaves got in from the fields at night, the womans cooked supper whilst the mens chopped wood. Lessen the crops was in the grass mighty bad or something else awful urgent, there warn't no work done after dinner on Saturdays. The old folks ironed, cleaned house, and the like, and the young folks went out Saturday nights and danced to the music what they made beating on tin pans. Sundays, youngsters went to the woods and hunted hickory nuts and muscadines. The old folks stayed home and looked one another's heads over for nits and lice. Whenever they found anything, they mashed it twixt they finger and thumb and went ahead searching. Then the womans wrapped each other's hair the way it was to stay fixed 'till the next Sunday.

Christmas us went from house to house looking for locust and persimmon beer. Chillun went to all the houses hunting gingerbread. Ma used to roll it thin, cut it out with a thimble and give a dozen of them little balls to each child. Persimmon beer and gingerbread! What big

times us did have at Christmas. New Year's Day, they raked up the horse and cow lots if the weather was good. Marster just made us work enough on New Year's Day to call it working, so he could say he made us start the New Year right.

Marse David had cornshuckings what lasted two or three weeks at a time. They had a general to keep them brash boys straight. The number of generals depended on how much corn us had and how many slaves was shucking corn. After it was all shucked, there was a big celebration in store for the slaves. They cooked up washpots full of lamb, kid, pork and beef and had collard greens that was worth looking at. They had water buckets full of whiskey. When them Niggers danced after all that eating and drinking, it warn't rightly dancing; it was wrestling.

Them moonlight cotton pickings was big old times. They give prizes to the ones picking the most cotton. The prizes was apt to be a quart of whiskey for the man what picked the most and a dress for the woman what was ahead. Them Niggers wouldn't take no time to empty cotton in baskets, just dump it out quick on bagging in the field.

They went from one plantation to another to quiltings. After the womans got through quilting and ate a big dinner, then they asked the mens to come in and dance with them.

Whenever any of our white folks' gals got married there was two or three weeks of celebrating. What a time us did have if it was one of our own little misses gitting married! When the day arrived, it was something else. The white folks was dressed up to beat the band, and all the slaves was up on their toes to do everything just right and to see all they could. After the preacher done finished his words to the young couple, then they had the sure enough wedding feast. There was all sorts of meat to choose from at wedding dinners—turkeys, geese, chickens, peafowls and guineas, not to mention good old ham and other meats.

Marse David and Miss Betsey took mighty good care of their Niggers, especially when they was sick. Dr. Bynam Bell, their oldest son, was a doctor but Miss Betsey was a powerful good hand at doctoring herself. She looked after all the slave womans. For medicines they give us asa-fiddy, calomel and castor oil more than anything else for our different ailments.

Us had been hearing first one thing and another about freedom might come, when one morning Mr. Will Bell, a patroller come riding on his horse at top speed through the rye field where us was at work. Us made sure he was after some poor slave, 'till he yelled out: "What you Niggers working for? Don't you know you is free as jay birds?" About that time the trumpet blowed for dinner and us fell in line a-marching up to the big house. Marse David said: "You all might just as well be free as anybody else." Then he promised to give us something to eat and wear if us would stay on with him, and there us did stay for about three years after the war. I was burnt up then, because I didn't have the privilege of riding behind Miss Betsey on old Puss no more when she went to meeting.

Interviewed by Sadie B. Hornsby at 258 Lyndon Avenue, Athens.

LONNIE PONDLY

I WAS BORN in Madison County, six miles from Danielsville about eighty years ago in 1857. I was a slave, but a happy one. My young Mistress and Marster's names were Nancy and John Lester. My father's master was Jimmie Nunn. My father would have to get a pass from Mr. Jimmie to come to see my mother. You see, they were on different plantations. He got to come to see my mother twice a week. If he slipped out without the pass the patrollers got after him and if he outrun them and got back to his master he was safe, but if he didn't he got a whipping. Twenty-five licks was what he would get.

My Mistress would not let anyone whip us. You ought to have heard us yell "Old Mistress." Out she would come. Her curse word was "Drat your infernal soul. You just want to beat my little Niggers to death," she would say. Then Miss Sallie would leave a-running.

Oh, we were the happiest little souls in the world. Old Miss would never consult a doctor. She was as good as any of them. When we got sick we didn't say stomach. We would holler "Old Mistress" and she would come a-running and ask, "What is the matter with my little Niggers now?" "My belly hurts," I'd say. She always kept some medicine made of chinaberry roots. "Now take this and Mistress will give you some candy."

My grandma was the cook. She would throw on a ten-foot pole and let it burn to ashes and then make pones of bread. She would then put them in the ashes and when they cooked a while she took the shovel and threw ashes over them. When they were done she taken them out, washed them and greased them. We would go to the bottoms and find mussel shells. That is where we got our spoons that we ate with. We had plenty to eat. Mistress and young Marster wanted their Niggers to grow up healthy like our father. He was a big healthy Nigger. They would say, "It ain't no trouble for a big healthy Nigger to get married."

I remember one time they was sending us out to hoe cotton. I decided I didn't want to go, so I pitched a big fit. Instead of hoeing the cotton I laid down and started grabbing it with my teeth. Marster came out and sent me to the house. He said I never would amount to nothing. He didn't let me go to the field no more that year. He thought I was sick.

There was plenty of potatoes, corn, wheat and everything else that is raised on a farm, but Marster would never raise over one bale of cotton. We had ox carts in those days. I can remember when it taken two weeks to go to Augusta and back with that bale of cotton. Shoes were brought back for us all. Mistress got a dress and the rest was brought back in money. I remember when he didn't have no gins, us little Niggers would pick out the seed with our hands. My mother would card it; my grandma would spin it. Young Mistress was the weaver, and she made all our clothes. We just wore one garment, a long dress. The only way I could tell the difference in my sister's clothes and mine was mine had a little yoke on it.

If our Marster and Mistess saw a big healthy Nigger it won't no trouble to get him married. It didn't make no difference, white or colored, if there was a wedding you could hear it all around: "Are you going to the broom jumping tonight?" Everybody would go. We had

straw brooms back in those days. One was fixed about the size around my arm and five feet long. It was laid down on the floor. Everybody would gather around. The man and woman that was going to marry would stand by the broom. The preacher would say to the man, "Do you take this woman to be you wife?" He says, "Yes." "Well, jump the broom." After he jumped, the preacher would say the same to the woman. When she jumped the preacher said, "I pronounce you man and wife." That's how all marriage ceremonies were then.

We used to go to the same church, colored and white. We would sit on one side, I would always go with my grandma. She would put her shoes on. When we left she would pull them off and go on home barefooted. The preacher made my Uncle Harry a deacon and when they served bread and wine Uncle Harry, a deacon, would come down the aisle and pass it around.

Us Niggers had to have a pass anywhere we went, church and all. They never kept you from going anywhere, but you had to have that pass and it read pass and repass. There would be twenty-five white men who were called patrollers, as I have told you before, and they would watch and could tell when one of the Negroes didn't have a pass—his feet just would not stay on the ground, 'cause he was so nervous.

When we had big dances the patrollers would be in the middle, us slaves would be on each end, and if the patrollers made a start to arrest one of the Niggers for disobedience we would always have a fire and one of us would dip up a shovel of hot coals and throw it at them. By the time they got through dodging the hot coals we would be gone home to our white folks.

I remember when the Yankees came through, some big Yankee come up to my pa and said, "I will give you my horse and blanket if you will show me all the old rich bugs." Pa said, "Wait, let me get my shoes."

Instead of putting on his shoes he run through the house and yelled, "Everybody turn loose the horses." All the Yankees horses were old broke down horses, and they would take ours.

If a man wore a vest the Yankees thought he had a watch. One big Yankee walked up to Uncle Harry and said, "Take off the vest." Another one said, "Let the damn fool alone; can't you see he has no watch." All the time Uncle Harry had it hid under the wood pile. Just as soon as Uncle Harry got a chance he threw his vest in the swamp. One Yankee walked up to Mistress and said, "I haven't got any money." The Yankee took his knife and cut Mistress' dress open and gold and silver went everywhere. It was awful.

Mr. Franklin was my Marster's older brother. The Yankees got him and hung him up by his toes. He would not tell where his money was. Then they hung him up by his neck; he could hardly whisper, still he would not tell them where his money was. The Yankee yelled at one of his men to bring him the auger. He got poor old Mr. Franklin down and started boring in his head. Mr. Franklin said, "Please don't kill me, I will tell, it is under a pile of rocks in the garden in an old trunk." They got all of poor old Mr. Franklin's money.

The Yankees made my mother cook fifteen bushels of peas and three middlins of meat. They didn't wait for them to get done. The peas just got hot and swelled. They taken them and left with all the good horses they could catch of ours and all the money they could find.

At the time of the surrender I began another life. I was ten years old. My father sent me to several different schools. We stayed on at the old plantation though; my father and mother could stay together now and they worked and we had plenty. Lots of the old Niggers were left without anything. My father would raise a bunch of hogs and put them in the cellar and sell them at a very high price. I can remember him selling

[88]

wheat at sixty dollars a bushel. He made a pair of raw hide shoes one time and sold them for one hundred dollars. This is something else I want to tell you. My father cut down maple trees and let them dry. Then he made little pegs and used them for nails to make his shoes. He was a very smart man.

Interviewed by Ina B. Hawkes in Athens in November, 1939.

ROBERT SHEPHERD

I WAS BORN on Marster Joe Echols' plantation in Oglethorpe County, about ten miles from Lexington, Georgia. Mammy was Cynthia Echols before she married up with my daddy. He was Peyton Shepherd. After Pappy and Mammy got married, Old Marse Shepherd sold Pappy to Marse Joe Echols so as they could stay together.

Marse Joe had three plantations, but he didn't live on none of them. He lived in Lexington. He kept a overseer on each one of his plantations and they had better be good to his Niggers, or else Marse Joe would sure get them away from there. He never allowed them to work us too hard, and in bad or real cold weather us didn't have to do no outside work except everyday chores what had to be done, come rain or shine, like milking, tending the stock, fetching in wood and things like that. He seed that us had plenty of good something to eat and all the clothes us needed. Us was lots better off in them days than us is now.

Old Marster, he had so many Niggers that he never knowed them all. One day he was a-riding along towards one of his plantations and he met one of his slaves, named William. Marse Joe stopped him and asked him who he was. William said: "Why Marster, I'se your Nigger. Don't you know me?" Then Marster, he just laughed and said: "Well, hurry

on home when you gits what you is gwine after." He was in a good humor that way most all the time. I kin see him now a-riding that little horse of his what he called Button, and his little fice dog hopping along on three legs right side of the hoss. There warn't nothing the matter with that little dog; walking on three legs was just his way of gitting around.

Marster never let none of the slave chillun on his plantation do no work 'till they got fifteen—that was soon enough, he said. On all of his plantations there was one old woman that didn't have nothing else to do but look after and cook for the Nigger chillun whilst they mammies was at work in the fields. Aunt Viney took keer of us. She had a big old horn what she blowed when it was time for us to eat, and us knowed better than to git so far off us couldn't hear that horn, for Aunt Viney would sure tear us up. Marster had done told her she better fix us plenty to eat and give it to us on time. There was a great long trough what went plum across the yard, and that was where us ate. For dinner us had peas or some other sort of vegetables and cornbread. Aunt Viney crumbled up that bread in the trough and poured the vegetables and pot liquor over it. Then she blowed the horn and chillun come a-running from every which away. If us ate it all up, she had to put more victuals in the trough. At nights, she crumbled the cornbread in the trough and poured buttermilk over it. Us never had nothing but corn-bread and buttermilk at night. Sometimes that trough would be a sight, because us never stopped to wash our hands, and before us had been eating more than a minute or two what was in the trough would look like the red mud what had come off of our hands. Sometimes Aunt Viney would fuss at us and make us clean it out.

There was a big sand bar down on the creek what made a fine place to play and wading in the branches was lots of fun. Us frolicked up and

down them woods and had all sorts of good times—anything to keep away from Aunt Viney because she was sure to have us fetching in wood or sweeping the yards if us was handy where she could find us. If us was out of her sight she never bothered about them yards and things. Us was scared to answer that horn when us got in Marster's tobacco. He raised lots of tobacco and rationed it out to men, but he never allowed chillun to have none 'till they was big enough to work in the fields. Us found out how to get in his tobacco house and us kept on gitting his tobacco before it was dried out 'till he missed it. Then he told Aunt Viney to blow that horn and call up all the chillun. "I'se going to whip every one of them," he would declare. After us got there and he seed that green tobacco had done made us so sick us couldn't eat, he just couldn't beat us. He just laughed and said: "It's good enough for you."

Aunt Martha, she done the milking and helped Aunt Nancy cook for the slaves. They had a big long kitchen up at the big house where the overseer lived. The slaves what worked in the field never had to do their own cooking. It was all done for them in that big old kitchen. They cooked some of the victuals in big old washpots and there was sure a plenty for all. All the cooking was done in big fireplaces what had racks made inside to hang pots on and they had big old ovens for baking and thick iron skillets and long-handled frying pans. You just can't imagine how good things was cooked that way on the open fire. Nobody never had no better hams and other meat than our Marster kept in them big old smokehouses, and his slaves had meat just like white folks did. Them cooks knowed they had to cook a plenty and have it ready when it was time for the slaves to come in from the fields. Miss Ellen, the overseer's wife, went out in the kitchen and looked over everything to see that it was all right and then she blowed the bugle. When the slaves heared

that bugle, they come in a-singing from the fields. They was happy because they knowed Miss Ellen had a good dinner ready for them.

The slave quarters was long rows of log cabins with chimneys made out of sticks and red mud. Them chimneys was all the time ketching fire. They didn't have no glass windows. For a window, they just cut a opening in a log and fixed a piece of plank across it so it would slide when they wanted to open or close it. Doors was made out of rough planks, beds was rough home-made frames nailed to the side of the cabins, and mattresses was coarse, home-wove ticks filled with wheat straw. They had good home-made kivver. Them beds slept mighty good.

There warn't many folks sick them days, especially amongst the slaves. When one did die, folks would go twelve or fifteen miles to the burying. Marster would say: "Take the mules and wagons and go but, mind you, take good care of them mules." He never seemed to care if us went—fact was, he said us ought to go. If a slave died on our place, nobody went to the fields 'till after the burying. Marster never let nobody be buried 'till they had been dead twenty-four hours, and if they had people from some other place, he waited 'till they could git there. He said it warn't right to hurry them off into the ground too quick after they died. There warn't no undertakers them days. The homefolks just laid the corpse out on the cooling board 'till the coffin was made. A cooling board was made out of a long straight plank raised a little at the head and had legs fixed to make it set straight. They wropt woman corpses in winding sheets. Uncle Squire, the man what done all the wagon work and building on our place, made coffins. They was just plain wood boxes what they painted to make them look nice. White preachers conducted the funerals, and most of the time our own Marster done it, because he was a preacher himself. When the funeral was done

preached, they sung "Harps From the Tomb"; then they put the coffin in a wagon and drive slow and careful to the graveyard. The preacher prayed at the grave and the mourners sung, "I'se Born To Die and Lay This Body Down." They never had no outside box for the coffin to be set in, but they put planks on top of the coffin before they started shovelling in the dirt.

Fourth Sundays was our meeting days and everybody went to church. Us went to our white folks' church and ride in a wagon behind their carriage. There was two Baptist preachers—one of them was Mr. John Gibson and the other was Mr. Patrick Butler. Marse Joe was a Methodist preacher himself, but they all went to the same church together. The Niggers set in the gallery. When they had done give the white folks the sacrament, they called the Niggers down from the gallery and give them sacrament too. Church days was sure enough big meeting days because everybody went. They preached three times a day; at eleven in the morning, at three in the evening, and then again at night. The biggest meeting house crowds was when they had baptizing, and that was right often. They dammed up the creek on Saturday so as it would be deep enough on Sunday, and they done the baptizing before they preached the three o'clock sermon. At them baptizings there was all sorts of shouting, and they would sing "Roll Jordan Roll," "The Living Waters" and "Lord I'se Coming Home."

When the crops was laid by and most of the hardest work of the year done up, then was camp-meeting time, along in the last of July and sometimes in August. That was when us had the biggest times of all. They had great big long tables and just everything good to eat. Marster would kill five or six hogs and have them carried thar to be barbecued, and he carried his own cooks along. After the white folks ate they fed the Niggers, and there was always a plenty for all. Marster sure looked

after all his Niggers good at them times. When the camp-meeting was over, then come the big baptizing: white folks first, then Niggers. One time there was a old slave woman what got so scared when they got her out in the creek that somebody had to pull her foots out from under her to get her under the water. She got out from thar and testified that it was the devil a-holding her back.

The white ladies had nice silk dresses to wear to church. Slave womans had new calico dresses what they wore with hoopskirts they made out of grapevines. They wore poke bonnets with ruffles on them and, if the weather was sort of cool, they wore shawls. Marster always wore his linen duster. That was his white coat, made cutaway style with long tails. The cloth for most all of the clothes was made at home. Marse Joe raised lots of sheep and the wool was used to make cloth for the winter clothes. Us had a great long loom house where some of the slaves didn't do nothing but weave cloth. Some carded bats, some done the spinning, and there was more of them to do the sewing. Miss Ellen looked after all that, and she cut out most of the clothes. She seed that us had plenty to wear. Sometimes Marster would go to the sewing house, and Mistress would tell him to get on away from thar and look after his own work, that her and Aunt Julia could run that loom house. Marster, he just laughed then and told us chillun what was hanging round the door to just listen to them womans cackle. Oh, but he was a good old boss man.

The big war was about over when them Yankees come by our place and just went through everything. They called all the slaves together and told them they was free and didn't belong to nobody no more and said the slaves could take all they wanted from the smokehouses and barns and the big house and could go when and where they wanted to go. They tried to hand us out all the meat and hams, but us told them us warn't hungry, because Marster had always done give us all us

wanted. When they couldn't make none of us take nothing, they said it was the strangest thing they had done ever seed and that that man Echols must have sure been good to his Niggers.

When them Yankees had done gone off Marster come out to our place. He blowed the bugle to call us all up to the house. He couldn't hardly talk, because somebody had done told him that them Yankees couldn't talk his Niggers into stealing nothing. Marster said he never knowed before how good us loved him. He told us he had done tried to be good to us and had done the best he could for us and that he was mighty proud of the way every one of us had done behaved ourselves. He said that the war was over now and us was free and could go any-where us wanted to, but that us didn't have to go if us wanted to stay there. He said he would pay us for our work and take care of us if us stayed or, if us wanted to work on shares, he would allow us to work some land that way. A few of them Niggers drifted off, but most of them stayed right thar 'till they died.

I stayed right on thar 'till after Marster died. He was sick a long, long time, and one morning Old Mistress, she called to me. "Robert," she said, "you ain't going to have no Marster long, because he's about gone." I called all the Niggers up to the big house and when they was all in the yard, Mistress, she said: "Robert, you been with us so long, you can come in and see him before he's gone for good." When I got in that room I knowed the Lord had done laid His hand on my good Old Marster, and he was a-going to that Home he used to preach to us Nig-gers about, and it appeared to me like my heart would just bust. When the last breath was done gone, I went back out in the yard and told the other Niggers, and there was sure crying and praying amongst them, because all of them loved Marster. That was sure one big funeral. Mis-tress said she wanted all of Marster's old slaves to go, because he loved

them so, and all of us went. Some what had done been gone for years come back for Marster's funeral.

Next day, after the funeral was over, Mistress, she said: "Robert, I want you to stay on with me because you know how he wanted his work done." Then Mistress' daughter and her husband, Mr. Dickenson, come thar to stay. None of the Niggers laked that Mr. Dickenson and so most of them left and then, about two years after Marster died, Mistress went to Atlanta to stay with another of her daughters, and she died thar. When Mistress left, I left too and come on here to Athens.

Interviewed by Grace McCune at 386 Arch Street, Athens, in July, 1938.

TOM SINGLETON

I WAS BORN in Lumpkin County on Marster Joe Singleton's place. My ma was named Nancy Early, and she belonged to Marster Joe Early what lived in Jackson County. My pa's name was Joe Singleton. I don't remember much about my brothers and sisters. Ma and Pa had fourteen chillun. Some of their boys was me and Isaac, Jeff, Moses, and Jack, and their gals was Celia, Laura, Dilsey, Patsey, Frankie, and Elinor. These was the youngest chillun. I don't remember the first ones. I don't recollect nothing at all about my grandma and grandpa, because us was too busy to talk in the daytime, and at night us was so whipped out from hard work us just went off to sleep early and never talked much at no time. All I knows about them is that I heared folks say my grandpa was one hundred seven years old when he died.

The slave quarters was in rows and had two rooms and a shed. They had beds made out of poles fastened together with pegs and across them was laid the slats what they spread the wheat straw on. Us had good cover because our Marster was a rich man and he believed in taking care of his Niggers. Some put sheets that was white as snow over the straw. Them sheets was boiled with home-made soap what kept them white like that. Other folks put quilts over the straw. At the end of the

slave quarters was the barns and cow sheds, and a little beyond them was the finest pasture you ever seed with clear water a-bubbling out of a pretty spring and running through it. Thar's where they turned the stock to graze when they warn't working them.

I plowed during the day on old Marster's farm. Some of the white folks what didn't have many Niggers would ask old Marster to let us help on their places at night. On bright moonshiny nights, I would cut wood, fix fences and such like for them. With the money they paid me I bought Sunday shoes and a Sunday coat, because I was a Nigger what always did like to look good on Sunday.

Us had good clothes the year around. Our summer clothes was white, white as snow. Old Marster said they looked like linen. In winter us wore heavy yarn what the women made on the looms. One strand was wool and one was cotton. Us wore our brogan shoes every day and Sunday, too. Marster was a merchant and bought shoes from the tan-yard. He had a colored man on his place what could make any kind of shoes.

I was four year old when Marster Dr. Joe Singleton died. All I re-members about him he was a big man, and I sure was scared of him. When he catched us in the branch, he would holler at us and say: "Come out of thar before you git sick." He didn't allow us to play in no water, and when he hollered, us lit a rag. There was about a thousand acres in Marse Joe's plantation, he owned a gold mine and a copper mine, too. Old Marster owned about sixty-five Niggers in all. He bought and sold Niggers, too. When Old Marster wanted to send news, he put a Nigger on a mule and sent the message.

After Marse Joe died, old Mistress run the farm about six years. Mistress' daughter, Miss Mattie, married Marster Fred Lucas, and old Mistress sold her share in the plantation then. My pa, my sister and

me was sold on the block at the sheriff's sale. During the sale my sister cried all the time, and Pa rubbed his hand over her head and face, and he said: "Don't cry, you is gwine live with young Miss Mattie." I didn't cry none, because I didn't care. Marse Fred bought us, and took us to Athens to live, and old Mistress went to live with her chilluns.

Marse Fred didn't have a very big plantation; just about seventy or eighty acres I guess, and he had about twenty-five Niggers. He didn't have no overseer. My pa was the one in charge, and he took his orders from Marse Fred, then he went out to the farm, where he seed that the Niggers carried them out. Pa was the carriage driver, too. It was his delight to drive for Marster and Mistress.

Marster and Mistress sure was good to us Niggers. Us warn't beat much. The only Nigger I remember they whipped was Cicero. He was a bad boy. My Marster never did whip me but once. Mistress sent me up town to fetch her spool of thread. I got to playing marbles and before I knowed it, it was dinner time. When I got home, Mistress was mad sure enough. Marster catched me and wore me out, but Mistress never touched me. I seed Niggers in the big jail at Watkinsville and in the calaboose in Athens. I seen plenty of Niggers sold on the block in Watkinsville. I recollects the price of one Nigger run up to $15,000. All the selling was done by the sheriffs and the slave marsters.

Marster Fred Lucas sold his place where he was living in town to Major Cook, and moved to his farm near Princeton Factory. After Major Cook got killed in the war, Marse Fred come back to town and lived in his house again.

They warn't no schools for Niggers in slavery time. Mistress' daughters went to Lucy Cobb Institute. Celia, my sister, was their nurse, and when all our little missies got grown, Celia was the house gal. So when our little missies went to school they come home and learned Celia how

to read and write. About two years after freedom, she begun to teach school herself.

Us had parties and dances at night. Sometimes Mistress let Celia wear some of the little missies' clothes, because she wanted her to out-shine the other Nigger gals. They give us a week at Christmas time, and Christmas day was a big day. They give us most everything: a knot of candy as big as my fist, and heaps of other good things. At corn shuck-ings Old Marster fetched a gallon keg of whiskey to the quarters and passed it around. Some just got tipsy and some got low down drunk. The onliest cotton picking us knowed about was when us picked in the daytime, and they warn't no good time to that. A Nigger can't even sing much with his head all bent down picking cotton.

Folks had fine times at weddings them days. Thar was more victuals than us could eat. Now they just hand out a little something. The white folks had a fine time, too. They let the Niggers get married in their houses. If it was bad weather, then the wedding was most generally in the hall, but if it was a pretty day, they married in the yard.

Old Marster and Mistress looked after their Niggers mighty well. When they got sick, the doctor was sent for straight away. They looked after them mighty well. Holly leaves and holly root boiled together was good for indigestion, and blackgum and blackhaw roots boiled together and strained out and mixed with whiskey was good for different miseries. Some of the Niggers wore little tar sacks around they necks to keep the fever away.

I was in the War about two years, with young Marster Joe Lucas. I waited on him, cooked for him, and went on the scout march with him, for to tote his gun and see after his needs. I was a bugger in them days!

I remembers I was standing on the corner of Jackson Street when they said freedom had come. That sure was a rally day for the Niggers.

About a thousand in all was standing around here in Athens that day. Yes Ma'am, the first time the Yankees come through they robbed and stole all they could find and went on to Monroe. Next to come was the guards to take charge of the town, and they was supposed to set things to going right. After the war I stayed on with Marse Fred, and worked for wages for six years, and then farmed on halves with him.

Interviewed by Sadie B. Hornsby at Athens.

NEAL UPSON

I WAS BORN on Marster Frank Upson's place down in Oglethorpe County, nigh Lexington, Georgia. Marster had a plantation, but us never lived there for us stayed at the home place what never had more than about eighty acres of land around it. What warn't raised on the home place, Marster had them raise out on the big plantation. Everything us needed to eat and wear was grown on Marse Frank's land.

Harold and Jane Upson was my Daddy and Mammy. Folks just called Daddy "Hal." Both of them raised right there on the Upson place where they played together whilst they was children. Mammy said she had washed and sewed for Daddy ever since she was big enough, and when they got grown they just up and got married. I was their only boy, but they had four gals older than me. They was Cordelia, Anne, Parthena and Ella. Ella was named for Marse Frank's onliest child, little Miss Ellen, and our little Miss was sure a good little child.

Daddy made the shoes for all the slaves on the plantation, and Mammy was called the house woman. She done the cooking up at the big house and made the cloth for her own family's clothes, and she was so smart us always had plenty to eat and wear. I was little and stayed

with Mammy up at the big house and just played all over it and all the folks up there petted me. Aunt Tama was an old slave too old to work. She was all the time cooking gingerbread and hiding it in a little trunk what set by the fireplace in her room. When us children was good Aunt Tama give us gingerbread, but if us didn't mind what she said, us didn't get none. Aunt Tama had the rheumatism and walked with a stick, and I could get in that trunk just about any time I wanted to. I sure did get about everything them other children had, swapping Aunt Tama's gingerbread. When our white folks went off, Aunt Tama toted the keys, and she evermore did make them Negroes stand around. Marse Frank just laughed when they made complaints about her.

In summertime they cooked peas and other vegetables for us children in a washpot out in the yard in the shade, and us ate out of the pot with our wooden spoons. They just give us wooden bowls full of bread and milk for supper.

Marse Frank said he wanted them to learn me how to wait on the white folks' table up at the big house, and they started me off with the job of fanning the flies away. Mistress Serena, Marse Frank's wife, made me a white coat to wear in the dining room. That little old white coat made me get the onliest whipping Marse Frank ever did give me. Us had company for dinner that day and I felt so big showing off before them in that white coat that I just couldn't make that turkey wing fan do right. Them turkey wings was fastened on long handles and after Marster had done warned me a time or two to mind what I was about, the old turkey wing went down in the gravy bowl, and when I jerked it out it splattered all over the preacher's best Sunday suit. Marse Frank got up and took me right out to the kitchen, and when he got through brushing me off I never did have no more trouble with them turkey wings.

Everybody cooked on open fireplaces them days. They had swinging racks what they called cranes to hang the pots on for boiling. There was ovens for baking and the heavy iron skillets had long handles. One of them old skillets was so big that Mammy could cook thirty biscuits in it at one time. I always did love biscuits, and I would go out in the yard and trade Aunt Tama's gingerbread to the other children for their share of biscuits. Then they would be scared to eat the gingerbread because I told them I'd tell on them. Aunt Tama thought they was sick and told Marse Frank the children weren't eating nothing. He asked them what was the matter, and they told him they had done traded all their bread to me. Marse Frank then asked me if I warn't getting enough to eat, 'cause he allowed they was enough there for all. Then Aunt Tama had to go and tell on me. She said I was worse than a hog after biscuits, so our good Marster ordered her to see that little Neal had enough to eat.

Them old cord beds was a sight to look at, but they slept good. Us corded lint cotton into bats for mattresses and put them in a tick what us tacked so it wouldn't get lumpy. Us never seen no iron springs them days. Them cords, criss-crossed from one side of the bed to the other, was our springs and us had keys to tighten them with. If us didn't tighten then every few days them beds was apt to fall down with us. The chairs was homemade, too, and the easiest-setting ones had bottoms made out of rye splits. Them oak-split chairs was all right, and some-times us used cane to bottom the chairs, but everybody liked to set in them chairs what had bottoms wove out of rye splits.

Colored folks went to church with their own white folks and set in the gallery. One Sunday us was all setting in that church listening to the white preacher, Mr. Hansford, telling how the old devil was going to get them what didn't do right. I just got to tell you about that day in the meeting house. A Nigger had done run off from his master and was

[105]

hiding out from one place to another. At night he would go steal his something to eat. He had done stole some chickens and had them with him up in the church steeple where he was hiding that day. When daytime come he went off to sleep. When he woke up Preacher Hansford was telling them about the devil was going to get the sinners. Right then an old rooster what he had stole up and crowed so loud it seemed like Gabriel's trumpet on Judgement Day. That runaway Nigger was scared because he knowed they was going to find him sure, but he warn't scared nothing compared to them Niggers setting in the gallery. They just knowed that was the voice of the devil what had done come after them. Them Niggers never stopped praying and testifying to the Lord, 'till the white folks had done got that runaway slave and the rooster out of the steeple. His master was there and took him home and give him a good, sound thrashing.

Them days it was the custom for masters to hire out what slaves they had that warn't needed to work on their land, so our master hired out two of my sisters. Sister Anna was hired to a family about sixteen miles from our place. She didn't like it there so she run away, and I found her hid out in our potato house. One day when us was playing she called to me right low and soft like and told me she was hungry and for me to get her something to eat but not to tell nobody she was there. She said she had been there without nothing to eat for several days. She was scared Marster might whip her. She looked so thin and bad I thought she was going to die, so I told Mammy. Her and Marster went and brought Anna to the house and fed her. That poor child was starved most to death. Marster kept her at home for three weeks and fed her up good, then he carried her back and told them folks what had hired her that they had better treat Anna good and see that she had plenty to eat. Marster was driving a fast horse that day, but bless your heart, Anna

beat him back home. She cried and took on so, begging him not to take her back there no more that he told her she could stay home. My other sister stayed on where she was hired out 'till the war was over and they give us our freedom.

Daddy had done hid all Old Marster's horses when the Yankees got to our plantation. Two of the riding horses was in the smokehouse and another good trotter was in the hen house. Old Jake was a slave what warn't right bright. He slept in the kitchen, and he knowed where Daddy had hid them horses, but that was all he knowed. Marster had give Daddy his money to hide, too, and he took some of the plastering off the wall in Marster's room and put the box of money inside the wall. Then he fixed that plastering back so nice you couldn't tell it had ever been tore off. The night them Yankees came, Daddy had gone out to the work house to get some pegs to fix something (us didn't have no nails them days). When the Yankees rode up to the kitchen door and found Old Jake right by himself, that poor old fool was scared so bad he just started right off babbling about two horses in the smokehouse and one in the hen house, but he was trembling so he couldn't talk plain. Old Marster heard the fuss they made and he come down to the kitchen to see what was the matter. The Yankees then ordered Marster to get them his horses. Marster called Daddy and told him to get the horses, but Daddy, he played foolish like and stalled around like he didn't have good sense. Them soldiers raved and fussed all night long about them horses, but they never thought about looking in the smokehouse and hen house for them and about daybreak they left without taking nothing. Marster said he was sure proud of my Daddy for saving them good horses for him.

Marster had a long pocketbook what fastened at one end with a ring. One day when he went to get out some money he dropped a roll of bills

that he never seen, but Daddy picked it up and handed it back to him right away. Now my Daddy could have kept that money just as easy, but he was an exceptional man and believed everybody ought to do right.

One time Marster missed some of his money and he didn't want to excuse nobody, so he decided he would find out who had done the devilment. He put a big rooster in a coop with his head sticking out. Then he called all the Negroes up to the yard and told them somebody had been stealing his money, and that everybody must get in line and march around that coop and touch it. He said that when the guilty ones touched it the old rooster would crow. Everybody touched it except one old man and his wife; they just wouldn't come near that coop where that rooster was a-looking at everybody out of his little red eyes. Marster had that old man and woman searched and found all the money what had been stole.

Mammy died about a year after the war, and I never will forget how Mistress cried and said: "Neal, your mammy is done gone, and I don't know what I'll do without her." Not long after that, Daddy bid for the contract to carry the mail and he got the place, but it made the white folks mighty mad, because some white folks had put in bids for that contract. They allowed that Daddy better not never start out with that mail, because if he did he was going to be sorry. Marster begged Daddy not to risk it and told him if he would stay there with him he would let him have a plantation for as long as he lived, and so us stayed on there till Daddy died, and a long time after that us kept on working for Old Marster.

White folks owned us back in the days before the war but our own white folks was mighty good to their slaves. They had to learn us obedience first, how to live right, and how to treat everybody else right; but

the best thing they learned us was how to do useful work. The onliest time I remember stealing anything except Aunt Tama's gingerbread was one time when I went to town with Daddy in the buggy. When us started back home a man got in the seat with Daddy, and I had to ride down in the back of the buggy where Daddy had hid a jug of liquor. I could hear it slushing around and so I got to wanting to know how it tasted. I pulled out the corncob stopper and took one taste. It was so good I just kept on tasting till I passed out, and didn't know when us got home or nothing else till I waked up in my own bed next day. Daddy give me a tanning what I didn't forget for a long time, but that was the worst drunk I ever was. Lord, but I did love to follow my Daddy.

A death was something what didn't happen often on our plantation, but when somebody did die folks would go from miles and miles around to set up and pray all night to comfort the family of the dead. They never made up the coffins till after somebody died. Then they measured the corpse and made the coffin to fit the body. Them coffins was lined with black calico and painted with lampblack on the outside. Sometimes they covered the outside with black calico like the lining. Coffins for white folks was just like what they had made up for their slaves, and they was all buried in the same graveyard on their own plantations.

When the war was over they closed the little one-room school what our good Marster had kept in his back yard for his slaves, but our young Miss Ellen learned my sister right on 'till she got where she could teach school. Daddy fixed up a room onto our house for her school and she soon had it full of children. They made me study, too, and I sure did hate to have to go to school to my own sister for she everymore did take every chance to lay that stick on me, but I expects she had a right tough time with me. When time come around to celebrate school commence-

ment, I was one proud little Negro, cause I never had been so dressed up in my life before. I had on a red waist, white pants and a good pair of shoes; but the grandest thing of all about that outfit was that Daddy let me wear his watch. Everybody come for that celebration. There was over 300 folks at that big dinner, and us had lots of barbecue and all sorts of good things to eat. Old Marster was there, and when I stood up before all them folks and said my little speech without missing a word, Marster sure did laugh and clap his hands. He called me over to where he was setting and said: "I knowed you could learn if you wanted to." Best of all, he give me a whole dollar. I was rich then, plumb rich.

Now, talking about frolicking, us really used to dance. What I means, is sure enough old-time break-downs. Sometimes us didn't have no music except just beating time on tin pans and buckets but most times Old Elice Hudson played his fiddle for us, and it had to be tuned again after every set us danced. He never knowed but one tune, and he played that over and over. Sometimes there was ten or fifteen couples on the floor at the same time, and us didn't think nothing of dancing all night long. Us had plenty of old corn juice for refreshment, and after Elice had two or three cups of that juice, he could get "Turkey in the Straw" out of that fiddle like nobody's business.

One time a houseboy from another plantation wanted to come to one of our Saturday night dances, so his master told him to shine his boots for Sunday and fix his horse for the night and then he could get off for the frolic. Abraham shined his master's boots 'till he could see himself in them, and they looked so grand he was tempted to try them on. They was a little tight, but he thought he could wear them, and he wanted to show himself off in them at the dance. They weren't so easy to walk in and he was afraid he might get them scratched up walking through the fields, so he sneaked his master's horse out and rode to the dance. When

Abraham rode up there in them shiny boots, he got all the gals' attention. None of them wanted to dance with the other Negroes. That Abraham was sure strutting 'till somebody run in and told him his horse had done broke its neck. He had tied it to a limb and sure enough, someway, that horse had done got tangled up and hung its own self. Abraham begged the other Negro boys to help him take the dead horse home, but he had done took their gals and didn't get no help. He had to walk twelve long miles home in them tight shoes. The sun had done rose up when he got there and it wasn't long before his master was calling, "Abraham, bring me my boots." That Negro would holler out: "Yes sir! I'm a-coming." But them boots wouldn't come off cause his foots had done swelled up in them. His master kept on calling and when Abraham seen he couldn't put it off no longer, he just cut them boots off his feet and went in and told what he had done. His master was awful mad and said he was a good mind to take the hide off Abraham's back. "Go get my horse quick, Negro, before I most kills you," he yelled. Then Abraham told him: "Marster, I knows you is going to kill me now, but your horse is done dead." Then poor Abraham had to out and tell the whole story and his master got to laughing so about how he took all the gals away from the other boys and how them boots hurt him that it looked like he never would stop. When he finally did stop laughing and shaking his sides he said: "That's all right Abraham. Don't never let nobody beat your time with the gals." And that's all he ever said to Abraham about it.

About the best times us had in the plantation days was the corn shuckings, log rollings and syrup cookings. Us always finished up them syrup cookings with a candy pulling. After he had all his corn gathered and put in big piles, Marster invited the folks from all around them parts. That was the way it was done: everybody helped the others get

the corn shucked. Nobody thought of hiring folks and paying out cash money for extra work like that. They elected a general to lead off the singing and after he got them to keeping time with the singing the little brown jug was passed around. When it had gone the rounds a time or two, it was a sight to see how fast them Negroes could keep time to that singing. They could do all sorts of double time then when they had swigged enough liquor. When the corn was all shucked they feasted and then drunk more liquor and danced as long as they could stand up. The log rollings and candy pullings ended the same way. They was sure grand good times.

I farmed with the white folks for thirty-two years and never had no trouble with nobody. Us always settled up fair and square and in crop time they never bothered to come around to see what Neal was doing, because they knowed this Negro was working all right. They was all mighty good to me. After I got so old I couldn't run a farm no more I worked in the white folks' gardens and tended their flowers.

Interviewed by Ina B. Hawkes at Athens.

GEORGE WOMBLE

I WAS BORN in the year of 1843 near the present site of what is now known as Clinton, Georgia. The names of my parents were Patsy and Raleigh Ridley. I never saw my father as he was sold before I was old enough to recognize him as being my father. I was still quite young when my mother was sold to a plantation owner who lived in New Orleans. As she was being put on the wagon to be taken away I heard her say, "Let me see my poor child one more time because I know I'll never see him again." That was the last I ever saw or heard of her. As I had no brothers or sisters or any other relatives to care for me my master, who was Mr. Robert Ridley, had me placed in his house where I was taught to wait tables and to do all kinds of house work. Mr. Ridley had a very large plantation and he raised corn, cotton, oats, wheat, peas and live stock. Horses and mules were his specialty. I remember that he had one little boy whose job was to break these animals so that they could be easily sold. My job was to wait tables, help with the house cleaning and to act as nurse maid to three young children belonging to the master. At other times I drove the cows to and from the pasture and I often helped with the planting in the fields when the field hands were rushed. Out of the forty-odd slaves that were held by

the Ridleys all worked in the field with the exception of myself and the cook, whose name was Harriet Ridley.

I believe that Mr. Ridley was one of the meanest men that ever lived. Sometimes he whipped us, especially us boys, just to give himself a little fun. He would tie us in such a way as to cause our bodies to form an angle and then he proceeded to use the whip. When he had finished he would ask: "Who do you belong to?" And we had to answer, "Marse Robert." At other times he would throw us in a large tank that held about two thousand gallons of water. He then stood back and laughed while we struggled to keep from drowning.

When Marse Robert died I was still a small boy. Several months after his death Mrs. Ridley gave the plantation up and took her share of the slaves (ten in number) and moved to Talbert County near the present location of Talbotton, Georgia. The other slaves and the plantation were turned over to Marse Robert's relatives. After a few months stay in this place I was sold to Mrs. Ridley's brother, Enoch Womble. On the day that I was sold three doctors examined me and I heard one of them say, "This is a thoroughbred boy. His teeth are good and he has good muscles and eyes. He'll live a long time." Then Mr. Womble said, "He looks intelligent, too. I think I'll take him and make a blacksmith out of him." And so to close the deal he paid his sister five hundred dollars for me.

The slaves all got up long before day and prepared their breakfasts and then before it was light enough to see clearly they were standing in the field holding their hoes and other implements—afraid to start work for fear that they would cover the cotton plants with dirt because they couldn't see clearly due to the darkness. An overseer was hired by the master to see that the work was done properly. If any of the slaves were careless about their work they were made to take off their clothes in the

field before all the rest, and then a sound whipping was administered. Field hands also got whippings when they failed to pick the required 300 pounds of cotton daily. To avoid a whipping for this they sprinkled the white sand of the fields on the dew-soaked cotton and at the time it was weighed they were credited with more pounds than they had actually picked. Around ten or eleven o'clock in the morning they were all allowed to go to the cook house where they were given dinner by the plantation cook. By one o'clock they were all back in the field where they remained until it was too dark to see clearly, and then they were dismissed by the overseer after he had checked the number of pounds of cotton that they had picked.

The slaves knew that whenever Mr. Womble hired a new overseer he was always told that if he couldn't handle the slaves his services would not be needed. The cook had heard the master tell a prospective overseer this and so whenever a new one was hired the slaves were quick to see how far they could go with him. An overseer had to be a very capable man in order to keep his job as overseer on the Womble plantation because if the slaves found out that he was afraid of them fighting him (and they did sometimes) they took advantage of him so much so that the production dropped and the overseer either found himself trying to explain to his employer or else looking for another job. The master would never punish a slave for beating an overseer with his fists.

During rainy weather the slaves shucked corn, piled manure in the barns, and made cloth. In the winter season the men split rails, built fences and dug ditches, while the women did the weaving and the making of cloth. Those slaves who were too old to work in the field remained at home where they nursed the sick slaves and attended to the needs of those children who were too young for field work. Those children who were still being fed from their mother's breasts were also

under the care of one of these old persons. However, in this case the mothers were permitted to leave the field twice a day (once between breakfast and dinner and once between dinner and supper) so that these children could be fed.

At times Mr. Womble hired some of his slaves out to work by the day for some of the other nearby plantation owners. I was often hired out to the other white ladies of the community to take care of their children and to do their housework. Because of my ability to clean a house and to handle children I was in constant demand.

The men worked every day in the week while the women were given Saturday afternoon off so that they might do their personal work like the washing and the repairing of the single men's clothing in addition to their own. No night work was required of any of them except during the winter when they were given three cuts of thread to card, reel and spin each night.

There were some days when the master called them all to his back yard and told them that they could have a frolic. While they danced and sang the master and his family sat and looked on. On days like the Fourth of July and Christmas in addition to the frolic barbecue was served.

Clothes were given to all the slaves once a year. An issue for the men usually consisted of one or two pairs of pants and some shirts, underwear, woolen socks and a pair of heavy brogans that had been made of horse hide. These shoes were reddish in appearance and were as stiff as boards. For special wear the men were given a garment that was made into one piece by sewing the pants and shirt together. This was known as a "roundabout." The women were given one or two dresses that had been made of the same material as that of the men's pants. As the cloth that these clothes were made of was very coarse and heavy most of them

lasted until the time for the next issue. None of the clothing that the slaves wore was bought. After the cloth had been made by the slaves who did all the spinning and the weaving the master's wife cut the clothes out while the slave women did the sewing. One of the men was a cobbler and it was he who made all of the shoes for slave use. In the summer months the field hands worked in their bare feet regardless of whether they had shoes or not. I was fifteen years old when I was given my first pair of shoes. They were a pair of red boots and were so stiff that I needed help to get them on my feet as well as to get them off. Once when the master had suffered some few financial losses the slaves had to wear clothes that were made of crocus material. The children wore sacks after holes had been cut out for their heads and arms. This garment looked like a slightly lengthened shirt in appearance. A dye made of red clay was used to give color to these clothes. The bed clothing consisted of bagging sacks and quilts that were made out of old clothes.

At the end of the week all the field hands met in the master's backyard where they were given food for the week. Such an issue was made up of three pounds of fat meat, one peck of meal and one quart of black molasses. If their food gave out before the time for another issue they waited until night and then one or two of them would go to the millhouse where the flour and the meal was kept. After they had succeeded in getting in they would take an auger and bore a hole in the barrel containing the meal. One held the sack while the other took a stick and worked it around in the opening made by the auger so as to made the meal flow freely. After their bags were filled the hole was stopped up and a hasty departure was made. Sometimes when they wanted meat they either went to the smoke house and stole a ham or else they would go to the pen where the pigs were kept and take a small pig out. When they got to the woods with this animal they proceeded to skin and clean

it. All the parts that they did not want were either buried or thrown in the nearby river. After going home all of this meat was cooked and hidden. As there was danger in being caught none of this stolen meat was ever fried because there was more danger of the odor of frying meat going farther away than that odor made by meat being boiled.

The slaves were taught to steal by their masters. Sometimes they were sent to the nearby plantations to steal chickens, pigs and other things that could be carried away easily. At such times the master would tell them that he was not going to mistreat them and that he was not going to allow anyone else to mistreat them and that by taking the above mentioned things they were helping him to be more able to take care of them.

At breakfast the field hands ate fried meat, corn bread and molasses. When they went to the house for dinner they were given some kind of vegetable along with pot liquor and milk. When the day's work was done and it was time for the evening meal there was the fried meat again with the molasses and the corn bread. They ate this kind of food every day in the week. The only variation was on Sunday when they were given the seconds of the flour and a little more molasses so that they might make a cake. No other sweetening was used except molasses.

The cook and I fared better since we ate the same kind of food that the master and his family did. I used to take biscuits from the dishes that were being sent to the master's table. I was the waiter and this was an easy matter. Later I took some of these biscuits and sold them to the other little boys for a nickel each. Neither the master nor the slaves had real coffee. They all drank a type of beverage that had been made by parching bran or meal and then boiled in water.

The younger children were fed from a trough that was twenty feet in length. At meal time each day the master would come out and super-

vise the cook whose duty it was to fill the trough with food. For breakfast the milk and bread was all mixed together in the trough by the master who used his walking cane to stir it with. At dinner and supper the
children were fed pot liquor and bread and sometimes milk that had
been mixed together in the same manner. All stood back until the master had finished stirring the food and then at a given signal they dashed
to the trough where they began eating with their hands. Some even put
their mouths in the trough and ate. There were times when the master's
dogs and some of the pigs that ran round the yard all came to the
trough to share these meals. They were not permitted to strike any of
these animals so as to drive them away and so they protected their faces
from the tongues of the intruders by placing their hands on the sides of
their faces as they ate. During the meal the master walked from one end
of the trough to the other to see that all was as it should be. Before I
started to work in the master's house I ate with the other children for a
short time. Some of the times I did not have enough food to eat and so
when the time came to feed the cows I took a part of their food (a mixture of cotton seed, collard stalks, and small ears of corn) and ate it
when night came. When I started working in the house regularly I
always had sufficient food from then on.

For those who worked in the fields, log cabins were provided, some
distance behind the master's house. They were two-roomed buildings
made out of logs and daubed with mud to keep the weather out. At one
end there was a chimney that was made out of dried mud, sticks and
stones. The fireplace was about five or six feet in length and on the inside of it there were some hooks to hang the pots from when there was
cooking to be done. There was only one door and this was the front one.
They wouldn't put a back door in a cabin because it would be easy for a
slave to slip out of the back way if the master or the overseer came to

punish an occupant. There were one or two small openings cut in the back so that they could get air.

The furniture was made by the blacksmith. In one corner of the room there was a large bed that had been made out of heavy wood. Rope that ran from side to side served as the springs while the mattress was a large bag that had been stuffed with wheat straw. The only other furnishings were a few cooking utensils and one or two benches. As many as four families lived in one of these cabins although the usual number to a cabin was three families. There was one other house where the young children were kept while their parents worked in the fields.

Most of the sickness on the Womble plantation was due to colds and fever. For the treatment of either of these ailments the master always kept a large can filled with a mixture of turpentine and castor oil. When anyone complained of a cold a dose of this oil was prescribed. The master gave this dose from a very large spoon that always hung from the can. The slaves also had their own home made remedies for the treatment of different ailments. Yellow root tea and black-hall tea were used in the treatment of colds while willow tea was used in the treatment of fever. Another tea made from the droppings of sheep was used as a remedy for the measles. A doctor was always called when anyone was seriously ill. He was always called to attend those cases of childbirth. Unless a slave was too sick to walk he was required to go to the field and work like the others. If, however, he was confined to his bed a nurse was provided to attend to his needs.

None of the slaves ever had the chance to learn how to read and write. Sometimes the young boys who carried the master's children's books to and from school would ask these children to teach them to write but as they were afraid of what their father might do they always refused. On the adjoining plantation the owner caught his son teaching

a little slave boy to write. He was furious and after giving his son a very severe beating he then cut off the thumb and forefinger of the slave. The only things that were taught the slaves was the use of their hands.

When a male slave reached the age of twenty-one he was allowed to court. The same was true of a girl that had reached the age of eighteen. If a couple wished to marry they had to get permission from the master who asked each in turn if they wished to be joined as man and wife and if both answered that they did they were taken into the master's house where the ceremony was performed. A broom was placed in the center of the floor and the couple was told to hold hands. After joining hands they were commanded to jump over the broom and then to turn around and jump back. After this they were pronounced man and wife. A man who was small in stature was never allowed to marry a large, robust woman. Sometimes when the male slaves on one plantation were large and healthy looking and the women slaves on some nearby plantation looked like they might be good breeders the two owners agreed to allow the men belonging to the one to visit the women belonging to the other; in fact they encouraged this sort of thing in hopes that they would marry and produce big healthy children. In such cases passes were given freely.

There was always a great amount of whipping on this plantation. This was practically the only form of punishment used. Most of them were whipped for being disobedient or for being unruly. I heard my master say that he would not have a slave that he could not rule and to be sure that the slaves held him and his family in awe he even went so far as to make all of them go and pay their respects to the newly born white children on the day after their birth. At such a time they were required to get in line outside the door and then one by one they went through the room and bowed their heads as they passed the bed and

said, "Young Marster" or if the baby was a girl they said, "Young Mistress." On one occasion I saw my master and a group of other white men beat an unruly slave until his back was raw and then a red hot iron bar was applied to his back. Even this did not make the slave submissive because he ran away immediately afterwards. After this treatment many slaves ran away, especially on the Ridley plantation. Some were caught and some were not. One of the slaves on the Womble plantation took his wife and ran away. He and his wife lived in a cave that they found in the woods and there they raised a family.

I was whipped to such an extent by my master, who used a walking cane, that I had no feeling in my legs. One other time I was sent off by the master and instead of returning immediately I stopped to eat persimmons. The master came upon me at the tree and started beating me on the head with a wagon spoke.

Several years before the war I was sold to Mr. Jim Womble, the son of Mr. Enoch Womble. He was as mean as his father or meaner. The first thing that I remember in regard to the war was to hear my master say that he was going to join the army and bring Abe Linclon's head back for a soap dish. He also said that he would wade in blood up to his neck to keep the slaves from being freed. The slaves would go to the woods at night where they sang and prayed. Some used to say: "I knew that some day we'll be free and if we die before that time our children will live to see it."

When the Yankees marched through they took all of the silver and gold that had been hidden in the wall on the Womble plantation. They also took all of the livestock on the plantation, most of which had been hidden in the swamps. These soldiers then went into the house and tore the beds up and poured syrup in the mattresses. At the time all of the white people who lived on the plantation were hiding in the woods.

After the soldiers had departed, taking those slaves along who wished to follow, Mrs. Womble went back into the house and continued to make the clothes and the bandages that were to be used by the Confederate soldiers.

Interviewed by Elizabeth Driskell in Columbus in January, 1937.

APPENDIX

SELECTIONS FROM FURTHER INTERVIEWS

LIVING QUARTERS

The cabins that the slaves occupied were located on one section of the plantation known as the quarters. These dwellings were crude one-roomed structures usually made from logs. In order to keep the weather out, mud was used to close the openings between the logs. In most instances the furnishing of a cabin was complete after a bed, a bench and a few cooking utensils had been placed in it. As there were no stoves for slave use, all cooking was done at the fireplace, which, like the chimney, was made of mud and stones. One or two openings served the purpose of windows, and shutters were used instead of glass. The mattresses on which they slept were made from hay, grass or straw. When a light was needed a tallow candle or a pine knot was lighted.[1]*

I knows us lived in log houses what had great big chimneys made out of sticks and mud. Why, them fireplaces was about eight feet wide, and you could put a whole stick of cord wood on the fire. Us slept on high-up beds what had big posts and instead of springs, they had stout cords

* For numbered references see pp. 165–6.

[125]

wove across to hold the mattress. The last time I slept on one of them sort of beds was when I was a little boy, sleeping with my Ma.[2]

Approximately one block from the planter's home, the quarters were clustered. There were numerous log houses with stick chimneys in which the slave families dwelt. They were composed of one room, sparsely furnished. The beds were corded with rope and as large families were encouraged, it was often necessary for several members to sleep on the floor. There was an open fireplace at which family meals were prepared. The equipment consisted of an iron pot suspended by a hanger and a skillet with long legs that enabled the cook to place fire beneath it.[3]

Then I live in a cabin like the rest of the Niggers. The quarters was stretched out in a line behind Marse Jim's house. Every Nigger family had a house to themselves. Me and my Pa and Ma lived in a cabin with my sisters. Their names was Saphronia and Annie. We had beds in them cabins made out of cypress. Everybody cooked on the fireplace. They had pots and boilers that hung over the fire and we put the victuals in there and they cooked and we ate them. Of course we never ate so much in the cabin because every morning the folks all went to the field. Ma and Pa was field hands, and I worked there, too, when I got big enough.[4]

FOOD

Us had everything good to eat. Marse Thomas was a rich man and fed his Niggers well. They cooked in a big open fireplace and boiled greens and some of the other victuals in a great big pot what swung on a rack. Meat, fish and chickens was fried in a griddle iron what was set on a flat-topped trivet with slits to let the fire through. Hoe cakes made of cornmeal and wheat flour sure was good cooked on that griddle. 'Taters

was roasted in the ashes, and they cooked bread what they called ash cake in the coals.[5]

Slaves were required to prepare their own meals three times a day. This was done in a big open fireplace which was filled with hot coals. The master did not give them much of a variety of food, but allowed each family to raise their own vegetables. Each family was given a hand-out of bacon and meal on Saturdays; and through the week, corn ash cakes and meat which had been broiled on the hot coals was the usual diet found in each home. The diet did not vary even at Christmas: only a little fruit was added.[6]

The food was given out every Monday night and had to last for a week. Each family cooked its own food. For an ordinary dinner, they had turnips, meat, syrup, biscuits and ashcakes made of meal. On Sundays they were given chicken or duck and cake. For holiday dinners they generally had barbecued goat or pig, biscuits and a plenty cake.

As the master's place was near a creek, the slaves were allowed to fish—generally at night, when they would build a big fire on the bank and fish for hours. The fish was then carried to their cabins and cooked the next day. Whenever the master wanted to hunt he would take his sons, some of the neighbor boys and a few of the slaves. They would hunt all night for 'possum, coon and fox. Dogs would be carried along to tree the animals.[7]

Oh! Us had plenty 'possums. Pappy used to catch so many sometimes he just put them in a box and let us eat them when us got ready. 'Possums tasted better after they was put in a box and fattened awhile. Us didn't have many rabbits. Us chillun used to go fishing in Moore's Branch. One would stand on one side of the branch with a stick, and one on the other side would roust the fishes out. When they came to the top and jump up, us would hit them over the head, and the grown folks

[127]

would cook them. There warn't but one garden, but that had plenty in it for everybody.[5]

We had enough for anybody. The victuals was cooked in great big pots over the fire just like they was cooking for stock—peas in this pot, greens in that one. Cornbread was made up and put back in the husks and cooked in the ashes. They called that an ash cake. Well, when everything was done the victuals was poured in a trough and we all ate. We had spoons cut out of wood that we ate with. There was a big lake on the plantation where we could fish and they sure was good when we had them for supper. Sometimes we go hunting and then we had 'possum and squirrel to eat. The 'possums was best of all.[4]

My Grandma, Nancy, was the cook and she fed all the little ones in the big ole kitchen what sat out in the yard. She had a tray she put our victuals on and what good things we had to eat and a plenty of everything! Us ate just what our white folks had: they didn't make no difference in us when it come to eating.

The first thing I recollects is being around in the kitchen when they was making finger cakes and my Mistress giving me the pan she made them in for me to sop it out. They ain't nothing what smells good like the cooking in them days.[8]

Sometimes those that had families wanted to cook in their own cabins so they was given enough food every Sunday morning to last a week. But if it give out, they could get some more. At dinner we'd most always have greens, peas, meat, potatoes, cornbread and syrup. But on Sundays we'd have biscuits. We always had plenty of something to eat. If we ever wanted fish, we could go fishing right on the place. We could hunt at night, but they wouldn't let us Niggers have guns. We'd hunt with dogs.[6]

We ate our breakfast while it was dark, and we trooped to the fields

at sun-up, carrying our lunch with us. Nothing fancy but just good rib-sticking victuals. We come in from the fields at sun-down, and there was a good meal awaiting us in the slave quarters. My good Marster gave out rations every second Monday.[9]

Imitation coffee was made by putting corn meal in a pan, parching it until it reached a deep golden brown and steeping it in boiling water. At noon, dinner was brought in the field in wash tubs placed on carts drawn by oxen. Dinner consisted of fat meat, peas and corn bread. Often all laundry was done in these same tubs.

The only time that this diet ever varied was at Christmas time when the master had all slaves gathered in one large field. Then several hogs were killed and barbecued. Everyone was permitted to eat as much as he could but was forbidden to take anything home. When someone was fortunate enough to catch a 'possum or a 'coon, he had a change of food.[10]

As a general rule all of the slaves on this plantation had enough food to keep them well and healthy. At the end of each week the field hands were given enough food to last them seven days. For most of them the week's supply consisted of three and one-half pounds of pork or fat meat, one peck of meal, flour and black molasses. The only meals that they had to prepare from these foods were breakfast and supper. Dinner was cooked in the plantation kitchen by one of the women who was too old for work in the fields. For this particular meal the slaves had some different type of vegetable each day along with the fat meat, corn bread and the pot liquor which was served every day. They were allowed to come in from the fields to the house to be served. Breakfast usually consisted of fat meat, molasses and corn bread, while supper consisted of pot liquor, bread and milk. The only variation from this diet was on Sunday when all were allowed to have biscuits instead of corn bread. If

anyone's food was all eaten before it was time for the weekly issue, it was just too bad for them because they would have to do the best they could until the time came to get more. When such a thing happened to anyone the others usually helped as far as their limited supplies would permit.[11]

The amount of food given each slave was also inadequate as a general rule. At the end of each week they all went to a certain spot on the plantation where each was given one peck of meal, one gallon of syrup and three pounds of meat. When hungry they made raids on the smokehouse. They increased their food by hunting and fishing. All meals usually consisted of grits, bacon, syrup, corn bread and vegetables. On Sundays and holidays they were allowed to have biscuits which they called "cake bread." The slaves made coffee by parching corn meal, okra seed or Irish potatoes. Syrup was used for all sweetening purposes.[1]

Food was distributed weekly in quantities according to the size of the family. A single man would receive on Sunday one peck meal, one quart syrup, three and a half pounds of meal and flour. Fresh meat was distributed on July 4 and Christmas. Peas, pepper grass, poke salad were plentiful in the fields. Milk and pot liquor could be had from the big house when wanted, although every family cooked for itself. Saturday afternoon was the general fishing time and each person might catch as many as he needed for his personal use.[3]

Chillun didn't have much to do. Us loved to hunt for turkey nests because they give us a teacake for every turkey egg us fetched in. Chillun ate in the yard at the big house, where they give us plenty of meat and corn bread with good vegetables for dinner. For breakfast and supper, us had mostly buttermilk and corn bread. On Sundays us had bread made from wheat flour and sopped good syrup with it. Sometimes Marse John would give us permission to kill little pigs at night and

broil them over the coals in our yards, and how us did enjoy them.[12]

I can see Mistress now a-riding up on her grey horse and carrying a basket on her arm plum full of biscuits. Mistress would say, "Where's them chillun, Mammy?" Lawdy, you never seed so many little Niggers pop up in all your life—just appeared like they come right out of the ground. Sometimes there would be so many chillun, she'd have to break the biscuits to make them go around and sometimes when she'd have an extra big basket, she'd say, "Bring on the milk and let's feed these chillun." A big bucket of milk would be brought, poured in little troughs, and they'd lie down on their stomachs and eat just like pigs! But they was just as slick and fat as you please. And clean, too. Old Mistress would say, "Mammy, you scrub these chillun and use that 'Jim Crow'!" That's a fine little comb what'll just naturally take the skin plum off your head along with the dirt.[13]

I was born and raised at Powers Pond Place and though I warn't but nine years old, I remember they had a nurse house where they put all the young chillun 'till they was old enough to work. They had one old women to look after us and our t'eat was brought to this house. Our milk was put on the floor in a big wooden tray and they give us oyster shells to eat with. All the chillun would gather around this tray and eat. They always let us eat 'till us got enough.[14]

CLOTHING

In summer time us wore checkered dresses made with low waists and gathered skirts, but in winter the dresses was made out of linsey-woolsey cloth and underclothes was made out of coarse unbleached cloth. Petticoats had bodice tops and the drawers was made with waists, too. Us chillun didn't know when Sunday come. Our clothes warn't no differ-

ent then from no other day. Us wore coarse, heavy shoes in winter, but in summer us went splatter bare feets.[5]

The house servants' houses was better than the field-hands'—and master used to buy us cloth from the Augusta factory in checks and plaids for our dresses, but all the field-hands' clothes was made out of cloth what was wove on mistress's own loom. Sometimes the poor white folks in the neighborhood would come and ask to make their cloth on mistress's loom, and she always let them. We had seamsters to make all the clothes for everybody, and mistress had a press-room, where all the clothes was put away when they was finished. When anybody needed clothes mistress would go to the press-room and get them.[15]

The cloth for the clothes was spun by some of the colored women. Every night each slave was given ten pounds of cotton to see. Then it was turned over to the women who spun it and finally passed on to the seamstress. After the clothes were made, the mistress took charge of them and distributed them among the slaves as she saw fit.[7]

Boys wore long blue striped shirts in summer and nothing else at all. Them shirts was made just like mother hubbards. Us wore the same thing in winter, only them shirts was made new for winter. By summer they had done wore thin. When the weather got too cold, Marster give us old coats, what grown folks had done most wore out, and us wasn't none too warm then with the wind a-sailing under our little shirt tails. Our shoes was rough old brogans what was hard as rocks, and us had to put rags inside them to keep them from rubbing the skin off our foots. Us didn't know what socks and stockings was then.[2]

Everybody wore the homespun cotton clothes that were made on the plantation by the slave women. The women wore striped ausenberg dresses while the men wore ausenberg pants and shirts that had been made into one garment. My clothes were always better than the other

little fellows, who ran around in their shirttails because I was always in the house. They used red clay to do the dyeing with. In the winter time cracked feet were common. The grown people wore heavy shoes called brogans while I wore the cast-off shoes of the white ladies. We all wrapped our feet in bagging sacks to help them to keep warm. We were given one complete outfit of clothes each year and these had to last until the time for the next issue.[11]

Clothing on the Ormond plantation was usually insufficient to satisfy the needs of the slave. Each year one issue was given each slave. For the men this issue consisted of one pair of brogan shoes, several homespun shirts, a few pairs of knitted socks and two or three pairs of pants. The brogans were usually made of such hard leather until the wearers' feet were usually blistered before the shoes were broken in. The women, in addition to a pair of shoes and some cotton stockings, were given several homespun dresses. Once I wore out my shoes before time for an issue of clothing. It was so cold until the skin of my feet cracked, causing the blood to flow. In spite of this my master would give me no more shoes. All clothing was made on the plantation except the shoes.[1]

MEDICINE

You usually weren't sick, but if you were sick, you got tea brewed from roots, herbs or whatnot. Turpentine was used for sore throats, cuts and bruises. Castor oil was used for everything else except a major fracture which called for the master bringing a doctor to the quarters.[16]

When us was sick, they give us herbs and things of that sort. In the springtime, they give us Jerusalem Oak seed in syrup for nine mornings and by then us was always rid of the worms. They attended to slave chillun so good and dutiful that there warn't many of them died, and

[133]

I don't never remember no doctor coming to my Mama's house.[12]

Marster had mighty good care took of his slaves when they got sick. There warn't many doctors in them days. They just used homemade medicines, mostly teas made out of herbs. I just can't get up no recollection of what herbs they did put in them teas. I does remember that chillun had to live with bags of assfiddy around their necks to keep off ailments. Ma give me and Bob, each one, a block of that assfiddy for good luck.[2]

We was well looked after. There was Nigger women on the plantation that was sorter nurses and if anybody got sick they'd tend to them. They'd make pepper and dogwood tea for them that had fever.[17]

When us was sick the white folks seed that we was tended to. They used to make Jerusalem Oak candy and give us. They took leaves of that bush an boiled them and then used that water they was boiled in and put sugar enough in it to make candy. And they used plenty of turpentine on us, too—plenty of it, and I believes in that today: it's a good medicine.[8]

Health of slaves was very important to every slave owner for loss of life meant loss of money to them. Consequently they would call in their family doctor if a slave became seriously ill. In minor cases of illness home remedies were used. In fact we used everything for medicine that grew in the ground. One particular home remedy was "Cow foot oil" which was made by boiling cow's feet in water. Other medicines used were hoarhound tea, catnip tea and castor oil. Very often medicines and doctors failed to save life, and whenever a slave died he was buried the same day. If he died before dinner the funeral and burial usually took place immediately after dinner.[6]

Medical care was promptly given a slave when he became ill. Special care was always given them, for the Willis family had a personal interest

in their slaves. On one occasion, the scarlet fever broke out among the slaves and to protect the well ones it became necessary to build houses in a field for those who were sick. This little settlement later became known as "shanty field." Food was carried to a hill and left so that the sick persons could get it without coming in contact with the others. To kill the fever, sticks of fat pine were dipped in tar and set on fire and then placed all over the field.[18]

Serious illnesses were not frequent, and home remedies compounded of roots and herbs usually sufficed. Queensy's light root, butterfly roots, scurry root, red shank root, bull tone root were all found in the woods and the teas made from them were cures for many ailments. Whenever an illness required a doctor, one was called.[3]

No doctor was called in to see the slaves when they were sick. I was born, growed up, married, had sixteen children and never had no doctor with me 'till here since I got so old. The white folks looked after their Negroes when they were sick. They were given tonics and things to keep them well, so sickness among them was rare. No store-bought medicines, but good home-made remedies were used. For instance, at the first sniffle they were called in and given a drink of fat lightwood tea, made by pouring boiling water over finely split kindling. That was because the lightwood got turpentine in it. In the spring there was a mixture of anvil dust—gathered up from around the anvil in the blacksmith's shop—and mixed with syrup, and a teaspoon full given every morning or so to each little black child, up in the white folks' yard. Sometimes instead of this, they were given a dose of garlic and whiskey, all to keep them healthy and well.[19]

Elderberry leaves good for baby rash and the bark good for fever; it really will cure it. For warts, you take nine grains of corn and pick that wart until it bleed and take that corn and get that blood on that corn,

and wrap it up and drop it in the street. Someone pick it up and they get your wart. Another way is to steal an Irish potato and put in your pocket.

For headache, Jimpson weed is good. Just take it and beat it up like a poultice and tie it around the head, and it will cure headache. Dairy vine leaves made into a poultice: really good. A string around the head, knotted in front, will draw out the pain. Salt on the mole of the head will stop headache. If you got headache, squeeze the head back and front or put vinegar and salt on brown paper and tie around the head.

For sore eyes, breast milk is good, and salt and water. If you get onion juice in your eye, look in the water and that will draw it out.

For measles, cornshuck tea is good. Mama use this here goat pills, made tea out of it and let them drink it. It tasted bad, but we had to take what mama give us. Put sugar in it to keep it from tasting so bad.

For mumps, fresh marrow from the hog's jowl will cure them. For swellings you boil mullein and pine tar and rub the swelling. Rusty nail water didn't help much. For fever and swellings a poultice of cow manure mixed with water and salt is good.

For cramps, I wears a brass ring on my finger or my wrist. Chicken manure tea is good for scarlet fever: you sweeten it just a little bit. When you get tetter-rash, just go out there and catch the dew and rub it over your face but you don't wash it off. If you got worms, take peach leaves and beat it in a poultice and bind it around your stomach and it will turn 'em downwards. I have done tried that. Peach leaves is good for constipation, too. You just cook the salad and eat it. I have done it many a time, it's fine. You put on the salad leaves and boil them, then put them in hot grease and fry them. And pokeberry wine is so pretty and fine for rheumatism.

Sulphur in your pocket will keep you from getting the smallpox. You

won't hardly pick up no kind of germs if you got sulphur on you. I always heard if you hang onion up in your house, it keep down fever, and I have tried it. When persons got smallpox, buzzard's grease is the best: stew it up in lard and take the fat.[20]

WORK

Marse John's son, Marse Willie Grant, blowed the bugle in the morning by four o'clock to get the slaves up in time to be in the fields by daybreak. When slaves got too old to work they took care of the chillun in a house down below the kitchen. Mamma worked in the field when she was able. Nobody on our place had to work in the fields on Saturday evenings. That was the time womans washed their clothes and cleaned up.[12]

Marster give the Niggers cotton patches and they could have what money they made to use for anything they wanted. My uncle made two bales every year besides the work he done for marster. Some of the Niggers raised poultry and then the white folks would buy them so they made money that way.[21]

On the plantation were a number of mills, among them the grist mill, used to grind corn, and tended by Uncle Nelson Browning. Uncle Nelson was also a carpenter. Uncle Joe Browning was a waggoner and attended to the stock on the plantation. The blacksmith shop on the plantation was operated by Uncle Bob Browning, who was a skilled blacksmith. The tannery was operated by Uncle Ben Browning. Leather for everyone's shoes was made by Uncle Ben. My father, Cicero Browning, was a shoe maker. Many a night I have held the light for my father to see by to make shoes for us. It was not necessary for master to have to buy anything for himself or his families, since plenty of food was raised

and each family had an ample amount of anything they desired. We even had a still from which the whiskey could be made.[22]

My grandfather owned a cotton patch, and the master would loan him a mule so he could plow it at night. Two boys would each hold a light for him to work by. He preferred working at night to working on his holidays. My master had a friend in Augusta, named Steve Heard, and just before my grandfather got ready to sell his cotton, the master would write Mr. Heard and tell him that he was sending cotton by Sam and wanted his sold and a receipt returned to him. He also advised him to give all the money received to Sam. When grandfather returned he would be loaded down with sugar, cheese, tea, mackerel for the family.[18]

When I was about eleven, I began toting water to the field hands. Then they started learning me to chop cotton. I soon began working there, too. I never did no house work 'till after freedom. One of my aunts cooked for the master and another was his house maid. He had several other maids, too. Marster give one of my sisters to his daughter when she married and we never saw her no more 'till we was all free.[19]

Every morning at four o'clock the overseer blowed a conchshell and all us Niggers knowed it was time to get up and go to work. Sometimes he blowed a bugle that'd wake up the nation. Everybody worked from sunup 'till sundown. If we didn't get up when we was supposed to we got a beating. Marster would make them beat the part that could buy. He never let them touch the part that couldn't be bought. In other words, slaves were whipped through their clothes.[4]

My master owned over a hundred grown slaves and the children were thick as blackbirds. Some worked in the master's house, some did the washing, others drove the horses and others did the same kind of work for the overseer. The majority of them helped in the tobacco fields. I worked there when I was about fourteen. My job was to pick the

worms off the leaves. If the overseer, when inspecting, would find a worm, he immediately called me and made me bite off its head. This was to make me more careful next time.[7]

I never worked as a slave because I wasn't old enough. In 1864, when I was nine years old, they sent me on a trial visit to the plantation to give me an idea of what I had to do someday. The place I'm talking about, where I was sent for a tryout, was on the outskirts of the town. It was a house where they sent chilluns out old enough to work for a sort of training. I guess you'd call it the training period. When the chilluns was near ten years old they had this week's trial to get them used to the work they'd have to do when they reached ten years. At the age of ten years they was then sent to the field to work. They'd chop, hoe, pick cotton and pull fodder, corn or anything else to be done on the plantation. I stayed at the place a whole week and was brought home on Saturday. That week's work showed me what I was to do when I was ten years old. Well, this was just before Sherman's march from Atlanta to the sea, and I never got a chance to go to the plantation to work again.[23]

Slaves on our place had a hard time. They had to work night and day. Marster had stobs all over the field to put lights on so they could see how to work after dark. The mens, more so than the womens, had to work every night 'till twelve o'clock. But they would feed them good. They had supper sent out in the field to them at about nine o'clock by a cripple boy who didn't do nothing but tote water and do things like that.[14]

Christmas was a great holiday on the plantation. There was no work done and everybody had a good time with plenty of everything good to eat. Easter was another time when work was laid aside. A big church service took place Sunday and on Monday a picnic was attended by all the Negroes in the community.

There were Fourth of July celebrations, log rollings, corn shuckings, house coverings and quilting parties. In all of these except the Fourth of July celebration it was a share-the-work idea. When a neighbor cleared a new ground and needed help, he invited all the men for some distance around and had a big supper prepared. They rolled logs into huge piles and set them afire. When all were piled high and burning brightly, supper was served by the fire light. Sometimes the younger ones danced around the burning logs. When there was a big barn full of corn to be shucked the neighbors gladly gathered, shucked the corn for the owner, who had a fiddler and maybe some one to play the banjo. The corn was shucked to gay old tunes and piled high in another barn. When a neighbor's house needed covering, he got the shingles and called in his neighbors and friends, who came along with their wives. While the men worked atop the house, the women were cooking a delicious dinner down in the kitchen. At noon it was served amid much merrymaking. By sundown the house was finished, and the friends went home happy.

The Fourth of July celebration marked the end of toil for a season. On the evening of the third of July all plows, gear, hoes and all such farm tools was brought in from the fields and put in the big grove in front of the house where a long table had been built. On the Fourth a barbecue was cooked; when dinner was ready all the hands got their plows and tools, the mules was brought up and gear put on them, and

then old Uncle Aaron started up a song about the crops was laid by and rest time had come, and everybody grabbed a hoe or something, put it on their shoulder and joined the march around and around the table behind Uncle Aaron. It was a sight to see all the hands and mules going around the table like that. Then when everybody was might nigh exhausted, they stopped and ate a big barbecue dinner. Us used to work hard to get laid by the Fourth so we could celebrate. It sure was a happy time on our plantations and the white peoples enjoyed it as much as us Niggers did.[24]

Oh, my Lord, frolics was what I loved. I didn't think heaven was as good as frolics. We'd have one on our plantation one Saturday night and next Saturday we'd have another one at some other plantation. We'd have them in the colored folks' cabins. One of the Niggers would pile all his things in one corner of the room and then we'd have a good place to dance. On Fourth of July and Christmas, Marster would give us the biggest kind of to-do. We always had more to eat than you ever saw on them days.[21]

We never worked none Christmas or the Fourth of July. Marster always give us big sacks full of fruit and candy on Christmas and a barbecue the Fourth of July. We never worked none New Year's Day neither. We just sat around and ate chicken, fish, and biscuits. During the week on Wednesday and Thursday night we had dances and then they was a lot of fiddling and banjo playing. We was glad to see days when we never had to work because then we could sleep.[4]

Christmas was something else. Us sure had a good time then. They give the chilluns china dolls and they sent great sacks of apples, oranges, candy, cake and everything good out to the quarters. At night during Christmas us had parties, and there was always some Nigger ready to pick the banjo. Marse Thomas always give the slaves a little toddy, too,

but when they was having fun, if they got too loud, he sure would call them down. I was always glad to see Christmas come. On New Year's Day, the General had big dinners and invited all the high-faluting rich folks.[5]

Once a week Mr. Heard allowed his slaves to have a frolic and folks would get broke down from so much dancing. The music was furnished with fiddles, which the slaves bought with money they earned selling chickens. At night slaves would steal off from the Heard plantation, go to LaGrange, and sell chickens which they had raised. Of course the masters always required half of everything raised by each slave and it was not permissible for any slave to sell anything.[6]

Frolics were common events on the Willis plantation, also quilting parties with good foods consisting of pies, cakes, chicken, brandied peaches. Dancing was always to be expected for everyone attending them. Our master always kept two or three hundred gallons of whiskey and didn't mind his slaves drinking. I can remember my master taking his sweetened dram every morning and often he gave me some in a tumbler. On Christmas Day big dinners were given for all the slaves and a few ate from the family's table after they had finished their dinner.[18]

There were many frolics in those days and other slaves would often attend, after getting permission from their masters. Dancing and singing were the main attractions. Before a frolic would begin the men would go to the swamps and get long quills, which would furnish music by blowing through them. This music reminded one of the music from a flute.[22]

Stretch cow-hides over cheese-boxes and you had tambourines. Saw bones from off a cow, knock them together and call it a drum. Or use broom-straws on fiddle-strings, and you had your entire band.[16]

Whenever anybody was late gitting his cotton picked out, he always give a moonlight cotton picking party. These parties was always give on moonshiny nights and was liked by everybody. After while they give everybody something good to eat, and at the end of the party, the person who had picked the most cotton got a prize. Sometimes they had pea shellings instead of corn huskings, but the parties and frolics was all pretty much alike.

At quilting bees, four folks was put at every quilt, one at every corner. These quilts had been pieced up by old slaves who warn't able to work in the field. Quiltings always took place during the winter when there warn't much to do. A prize was always give to the four which finished their quilt first. Refreshments went along with this too.

Cake walking was a lot of fun during slavery time. They swept the yards real clean and set benches around for the party. Banjoes was used for music making. The womens wore long, ruffled dresses with hoops in them and the mens had on high hats, long split-tailed coats, and some of them used walking sticks. The couple that danced best got a prize. Sometimes the slave owners come to these parties because they enjoyed watching the dance, and they decided who dance the best. Most parties during slavery time, was give on Saturday night during work seasons, but during winter they was give on most any night.

The men have even stole hogs from other people and barbecued them, then they would cook hash and rice and serve barbecue. The overseer knowed all about it but he eat as much as anybody else and kept his mouth shut. He was real good to all the slaves. He never run you and yelled at you like you warn't human. Everybody loved him, and would mind him better than they would anybody else. He always let the slaves shell corn 'till about ten o'clock, then everybody would stop and have supper. After that he would let them dance and play

games 'till twelve. Our master didn't say nothing about what the slaves done so long as the overseer was with them.[14]

PUNISHMENT

Mr. Brown was a fine person and never mistreated his slaves, although he did furnish them with the whip for infractions of rules such as fighting, stealing, visiting other plantations without a pass. One of the soundest thrashings I ever got was for stealing Mr. Brown's whiskey. My most numerous offense was fighting. Another form of punishment used in those days was the stocks, like those used in England. Serious offenses like killing another person were also handled by the master who might hang him to a tree by the feet or by the neck.[10]

Although I was never whipped, I have heard the whip being applied to my mother many times. It hurt me, because I had to stand back unable to help. When my mother got these whippings she always run off afterwards and hid in the woods which were nearby. At night she would slip to our cabin to get food and while there would caution me and the other children not to tell the master that they had seen her. The master's wife was very mean, and she was always the cause of these lashings.[1]

Mr. Browning never punished his slaves unnecessarily but on one occasion he lost his temper and whipped a woman unmercifully. Usually he performed the task of whipping with as much care and humanity as the nature of the case would permit. Since the Browning slaves were not restricted to any particular diet there was no need for anyone to steal; however, a woman known as Aunt Millie was caught stealing. Consequently he punished her until blood ran in streams down her back. There was very little whipping on the Browning plantation, and the patrollers were not allowed anywhere near.[22]

[144]

Punishment was seldom necessary on the Willis plantation as the master and mistress did everything possible to make their slaves happy, and to a certain extent indulged them. They were given whiskey liberally from their master's still and other special foods at special occasions. I remember once my Aunt Rachel burned the biscuits and the young master said to her: "Rachel, you nursed me and I promised not to whip you ever, so don't worry about burning the bread." My mistress was very fond of me, too, and gave me some of everything that she gave her own children, tea cakes, apples and the like. She often told me that she was my mother and was supposed to look after me. In spite of the kindness of the Willis family there were some slaves who were unruly; so the master built a house off to itself and called it the Willis jail. Here he would keep those whom he had to punish. I have known some slaves to run away on other plantations and the hounds would bite plugs out of their legs.[18]

I was never whipped by my master, but the overseer would often "clean me up." He would not stop the work to administer punishment but would promise me a whipping that night. With this promise in mind, I would run to the woods and there hide in safety. The overseer, for fear of losing one of the master's slaves and thereby losing his own job, would send slaves with torches to find me. By the time I had been found, the overseer would be so thankful that he would forget his promise and I would escape the punishment. All of the slaves were whipped by the overseer and not by my master.[7]

Mr. Heard was a very mean master and was not liked by any one of his slaves. Every morning my grandmother would pray, and old man Heard despised to hear anyone pray, saying they were only doing so that they might become free Niggers. Just as sure as the sun would rise, she would get a whipping. But this did not stop her prayers every

morning. This particular time grandmother Sylvia was in a family way and that morning she began to pray as usual. My master heard her and became so angry he came to her cabin, seized her and pulled off her clothes and tied her to a young sapling. He whipped her so brutally that her body was raw all over. When darkness fell her husband cut her down from the tree: during the day he was afraid to go near her. Rather than go back to the cabin she crawled on her knees to the woods and her husband brought grease for her to soothe her raw body. For two weeks the master hunted but could not find her; however, when he finally did, she had given birth to twins. The only thing that saved her was the fact that she was a mid-wife and always carried a small pen knife which she used to cut the cord of the babies. After doing this she tore her petticoat into two pieces and wrapped each baby. Grandmother Sylvia lived to be 115 years old.

Once grandmother Sylvia was told to take her clothes off when she reached the end of a cotton row. She was to be whipped because she had not completed the required amount of hoeing for the day. Grandmother continued hoeing until she came to a fence; as the overseer reached out to grab her she snatched a fence railing and broke it across his arms. On another occasion grandmother Sylvia ran all the way to town to tell the master that an overseer was beating her husband to death. The master immediately jumped on his horse and started for home, where he ordered the overseer to stop whipping the old man.[6]

All the Niggers worked hard. The cotton pickers had to pick 200 pounds of cotton a day and if a Nigger didn't Marse Frank would take the Nigger to the barn and beat him with a switch. He would tell the Nigger to holler loud as he could and the Nigger would do so. Then the old mistress would come in an say, "What are you doing, Frank?" "Beating a Nigger" would be his answer. "You let him alone; he is my

Nigger," and both Marse Frank and the whipped Nigger would come out of the barn. We all loved Marse and the Mistress.

If we went visiting we had to have a pass. If Niggers went out without a pass the patrollers would get him. The white folks were the patrollers and had masks on their faces. They looked like Niggers with the devil in their eyes. They used no paddles—nothing but straps with the belt buckle fastened on.

I got paddled one day. I left home on a Thursday to see a gal on the Palmer plantation five miles away. Some gal! I didn't get a pass. Everything was fine until my return trip. I was two miles out and three miles to go. There come the patrollers. I was not scared—only I couldn't move. They give me thirty licks. I ran the rest of the way home. There was belt buckle marks all over me. I ate my victuals off the porch railing.[9]

Once my Uncle William was caught off the Heard plantation without a pass and was whipped almost to death by the patrollers. He stole off to the depths of the woods, where he built a cave large enough to live in. A few nights later he came back to the plantation unobserved and carried his wife and two children back to this cave where they lived until after freedom. When found years later his wife had given birth to two children. No one was ever able to find his hiding place, and if he saw anyone in the woods he would run like a lion.[6]

To see that everyone continued working an overseer rode over the plantation keeping check on the workers. If any person was caught resting he was given a sound whipping. One day a young girl stopped to rest for a few minutes and my uncle stopped also and spoke to her. During this conversation the overseer came up and began whipping the girl with a sapling tree. My uncle became very angry and picked up an axe and hit the overseer in the head, killing him. The mistress was very

fond of my uncle and kept him hid until she could "run him." Running a slave was the method they used in sending a slave to another state to be sold again in order that he could escape punishment. You were only given this privilege if you were cared for by your mistress and master.

Overseers on the Ealey plantation were very cruel and whipped slaves unmercifully. My mother resented being whipped and would run away to the woods and often remained as long as twelve months at a time. When the strain of staying away from her family became too great, she would return home. No sooner would she arrive than the old overseer would tie her to a peach tree and whip her again. The whipping was done by a Nigger driver, who followed the overseer around with a bull whip especially for this purpose. The largest man on the plantation was chosen to be the Nigger driver.[25]

When I was about ten years old they started me toting water—you know carrying the water to the hands in the field. About two years later I got my first field job, tending sheep. When I was fifteen my old Missus give me to Miss Eva who married Colonel Jones. My young Missus was fixing to get married, but she couldn't on account of the war, so she brought me to town and rented me out to a lady running a boarding house. The rent was paid to my Missus. One day I was taking a tray from the outdoor kitchen to the house when I stumbled and dropped it. The food spill all over the ground. The lady got so mad she picked up a butcher knife and chop me in the head. I went running 'till I come to the place my white folks live. Miss Eva took me and wash the blood out my head and put medicine on it, and she wrote a note to the lady and she say, "Ellen is my slave, give to me by my mother. I wouldn't had this happen to her no more than to me. She won't come back there no more."

Old Mr. Miller had a man name Jolly, and he want to marry a woman off another plantation, but Jolly's master want to buy the woman to come to the plantation. He say, "What's fair for the goose is fair for the gander." When they couldn't come to no agreement the man he run away—he run away to the woods. Then they set the bloodhounds on him. They let down the rail fence so the hounds could get through. They search the woods and the swamps for Jolly but they never find him. The slaves they know where he is, and the woman she visit him. He had a den down there and plenty of grub they take him, but the white folks never find him. Five hundred dollars was what Miller put out for whoever get him.[26]

Teasing and playing pranks on the patrollers were favorite pastimes of some of the slaves. One of their choicest stunts was to tie a grape vine across some narrow, dark stretch of road where they knew the patrollers would pass. And, as the patrollers usually rode in a gallop, these vines would be sure to catch the foremost rider or riders somewhere between their saddle horns and necks and unhorse at least one of them.

The patrollers would break up the slaves' prayer meetings and whip all caught in attendance, unless a Nigger saved himself in flight. My father was once attending a prayer meeting in a house which had only one door. The slaves had turned a large pot down in the center of the floor to hold the sounds of their voices within. But, despite their precaution, the patrollers found them and broke in. Every Nigger present was "in" for a severe whipping. Thinking fast and acting quickly, my father stuck a big shovel in the fireplace, drew out a peck or more of hot ashes and cinders and flung them broadcast into the faces of these patrollers. The room was soon filled with smoke and the smell of burning clothes and white flesh and, in the confusion and general hubbub that followed, every Negro escaped.[27]

I ain't never heard nothing about no jails in slavery time. What they done then was almost beat the life out of the Niggers to make them behave. Ma was brung to Bairdstown and sold on the block to Marse Joe long before I was borned, but ain't nobody ever told you it was agin the law to learn a Nigger to read and write in slavery time? White folks would chop your hands off for that quicker than they would for almost anything else. That's just a saying, "chop your hands off." Why, a Nigger without no hands wouldn't be able to work much, and his owner couldn't sell him for nigh as much as he could get for a slave with good hands. They just beat them up bad when they catched them studying reading and writing, but folks did tell about some of the owners that cut off one finger every time they catched a slave trying to get learning.[28]

The overseer got us up about four o'clock in the morning to feed the stock. Then us ate. Us always stopped off by dark. There's a saying that you had to "brush" a Nigger in them days to make them do right. They brushed us if us lagged in the field or cut up the cotton. They could always find some fault with us. Master brushed us sometime, but the overseer most generally done it. I remembers they used to make the womans pull up their skirts and brushed them with a horse whip or a hickory; they done the mens the same way except they had to take off their shirts and pull their pants down. Niggers sure would holler when they got brushed.[29]

One time Marster got after one of his young slaves out in the field and told him he was a good mind to have him whipped. That night the young Nigger was telling an old slave about it, and the old man just laughed and said: "When Marster pesters me that way I just rise up and cuss him out." That young fellow decided he would try it out and the next time Marster got after him they had a rukus what I ain't never

going to forget. Us was all out in the yard at the big house, scared to get a good breath when us heared Marster tell him to do something, because us knowed what he was meaning to do. He didn't go right ahead and mind Marster like he had always been used to doing. Marster called to him again, and then that fool Nigger cut loose and he evermore did cuss Marster out. Lordy, Marster just fairly took the hide off that Nigger's back. When he tried to talk to the old slave about it the old man laughed and said: "Shucks, I always waits 'till I gets to the field to cuss Marster so he won't hear me."[30]

You go off to see somebody at night and if they catch you and you ain't got no pass then they going to whip you. You be glad to get away too because when they hit you, you was hit. I was down to old John Brady's place one night talking to a lady and old man Brady slipped up behind me and caught me in the collar and he say: "What you doing over here? I'm going to give you twenty-five lashes." And then he say to me: "Come here." He was just about as tall as I am and when I got to him he say turn around and I say to him that I ain't doing nothing and then he say: "That's what I'm going to whip you for because you ought to be home doing something." About that time when I stooped over to take off my coat I caught him in his pants and throwed him in a puddle of water and then I lit out for home. If you get home then they couldn't do nothing to you. He tried to chase me but he didn't know the way through the woods like I did and he fell in a gulley and hurt his arm. The next morning when I was hitching up the boss man's horse I seed him coming and I told the boss that he tried to whip me the night before and then the boss man say, "Did he have you?" I told him that he did, but that I got away. And then the boss say: "He had you and he didn't have you—is that right?" Then he say: "Don't worry about that. I can get you out of that. If he had you he should have whipped

you and that would have been his game, but he let you get away and so that was your game." About that time old man Brady had done got there and he told the master that I was on his place the night before and that I got away and when he tried to whip me and the master say to him: "That was his game—if you had him you should have whipped him. That's the law. If you had whipped him that would have been your game, but you let him get away and so that was his game." Old man Brady's face turned so red that it looked like he was going to bust.[31]

Slavery days was mighty hard. My master was good to us (I mean he didn't beat us much, and he give us plenty of plain food) but some slaves suffered awful. My aunt was beat cruel once and lots of other slaves, too. When they got ready to beat you, they'd strip you stark mother naked and they'd say, "Come here to me, God damn you! Come to me clean! Walk up to that tree, and damn you, hug that tree!" Then they tie your hands around the tree, then tie your feets; then they'd lay the rawhide on you and cut your buttocks open. Sometimes they'd rub turpentine and salt in the raw places, and then beat you some more. Oh, it was awful! And what could you do? They had all the advantage of you.[32]

They trained the hounds to run once a week. I was the house boy. The overseer tell me: "Squire, you go to such-and-such a place. Climb up that tree, way yonder." I would run on out and hide in the woods. Here after awhile the dogs come. I run around and fool them, then I climb the tree with the dogs and the overseer right on my track. Then the overseer call me down and I jump in the middle of the dogs, and he say: "Tickle him britches!" I play with the dogs and they love me. But when they was hunting people they was sure fierce.[33]

Our old master wasn't like some of the other masters in the community—he never did do much whipping of his slaves. One time I hit a

white man and old master said he was going to cut my arm off and that was the last I heard of it. Some of the other slaves used to get whippings for not working and for fighting. My mother got a whipping once for not working. When they got so bad old master didn't bother about whipping them—he just put them on the block and sold them like he would a chicken or something.[34]

The one to be whipped was tied across a log or to a tree and then his shirt was dropped around his waist and he was lashed with a cowhide whip until his back was raw. Whippings like these were given when a slave was unruly or disobedient or when he ran away. Before a runaway slave could be whipped he had to be caught and the chief way of doing this was to put blood hounds—Nigger hounds—on the fugitive's trail. I once saw a man being taken to his master after he had been caught by the dogs. His skin was cut and torn in many places and he looked like one big mass of blood. My father once ran away to escape a whipping during the Civil War, and he remained in hiding until the war was over with and then he was able to show himself without any fear.[35]

My grandmother said my grandfather used to slip off without asking for no pass. Sometimes the young bucks would bust in the smokehouse and steal roasting potatoes and broiling meat. The overseer come looking, and grandfather tore out to get home, but they whip the rest whatever they caught. They whip them bad—they raise a fence and put their head under the fence and whip them. Once they whip my grandmother. She was ploughing and mule go all right, but when it come back to this end, he would make a dart, and that would jerk the furrow crooked, and then she went around to see what make that dart, and a great big snake big as she, just rear up and look at her! She take the whip and cut him around the neck. Boss man come down there to see what the matter, because she quit working. She give him stiff talk, and

he whip her from one end of the road to the other, and the blood run down in her shoes, and she plying! I am so glad I ain't slave!

This fellow he wanted to go to see his sweetheart every night instead of just on pass night. He knowed he would get whipped if he got caught, so he went to the old voodoo man, the root worker, and asked him to help. The root man says: "I'll give you a piece of root to chew. When you face the boss man, you be talking and just a spitting, and the boss man can't put his hand on you." So he went there the next morning. The boss man in the blacksmith shop just a hammering down. He say: "Tom, what you doing so late?" Tom kept on a spitting. The boss man light in on him, and most beat him to death! Tom throwed that root just as far as he could and when he met the old voodoo man, he give him a good cussing, cause the voodoo wouldn't work.[20]

I seen many mens running away from the bloodhounds. Sometimes we chilluns be in the quarter playing, and a man would come running along fast, breathing hard, so skeered! The hounds be behind him. Then I can remember how they'd whip them when they catch him. They would make the men drop their pants and lay down across big logs and they'd whip him. The womens they'd drop their bodies and they'd whip them across the back and around the waists 'till the blood come.[36]

SALES

It was during cotton chopping time that year of 1860, a day I'll never forget, when the speculators bought me. Ma come home from the field about half after eleven that day and cooked a good dinner, I helping her. Oh, I never has forgot that last dinner with my folks. But, somehow I had felt, all the morning like something was going to happen. I

could just feel it in my bones. And sure enough, about the middle of the evening, up rode my young master on his horse, and up drove two strange white men in a buggy. They hitch their horses and come in the house, which scared me. Then one of the strangers said, "Get your clothes, Mary. We has bought you from Mr. Shorter." I commenced crying and begging Mr. Shorter to not let them take me away. But he say, "Yes, Mary, I has sold you, and you must go with them."

These strange men, whose names I ain't never knowed, took me and put me in the buggy and drove off with me, me hollering at the top of my voice and calling my Ma. Then them speculators begin to sing loud, just to drown out my hollering.

Us passed the very field where pa and all my folks was working, and I called out as loud as I could and as long as I could see them, "Good-by, Ma! Good-by, Ma!" But she never heard me. No, them white men was singing so loud Ma couldn't hear me. And she couldn't see me, because they had me pushed down out of sight on the floor of the buggy.

I ain't never heard tell of my Ma and Pa, and brothers, and sisters from that day to this.

My new owners took me to Baltimore, where they had herded together two two-horse wagon loads of Niggers. All of us Niggers was then shipped on a boat to Savannah, and from there us was put on the cars and sent to Macon and sold.[37]

Although nobody was ever sold on the plantation where I lived, I witnessed the selling of others on the auction block. The block resembled a flight of steps. The young children and those women who had babies too young to be separated from them were placed on the bottom step, those in their early teens on the next, the young men and women on the next, and the middle-aged and old ones on the last one. Prices decreased as the auctioneer went from the bottom step to the top

one, that is, the younger a slave was the more money he brought.[11]

They sold my mother. I didn't even know she gone, I so little and ain't know much, ain't got sense to miss her. She put me and my sister with one of our aunties and we stay there 'till freedom declared. My father was in Barnwell. My mother come back after freedom and got me and my sister, and went to Augusta and work with some white people.[38]

They had slaves in pens, brung in droves and put them in pens just like they was cows. They sold them by auctioning off to the highest bidder. I was only a child and never went around much. They put girls on the block and auctioned them off. "What will you give for this Nigger wench?" Lot of the girls was being sold by their master who was also their father, taken right out of the yards with their white chilluns and sold like herds of cattle. My sister was given away when she was a girl. She told me and ma that they'd make her go out and lay on a table and two or three white men would have sex with her before they'd let her up. She was just a small girl. She died when she was still in her young days, still a girl.[39]

When I was sixteen years old, Marster sold me and some more Niggers down South. Course us ain't want to go, but us have to. Us was chained together all the way from Norfolk to Savannah. And when us got there they put us in a stable pen right under where B. H. Levy's store used to be. The next morning was sale day. They brung us here for the Central Railroad. I was the only one not sold to the Central. They says I'se too young. Mister McAlpin he done wants me but the President of the road tell them that Doctor Arnold have done first pick to buy me. Doctor Arnold, he been the doctor for the railroad. Doctor Arnold, he want me for a house boy. Because Nellie, the doctor's wife, done spend some time in Virginia at Master Carter's home, and she know that I'se a first-class waiter on the table.

There was a pen under the Pulaski House where they lock up the Niggers whenever they got here in the night, and the man what have them in charge done stop at the hotel. The regular jail weren't for slaves, but there was a speculator jail at Habersham and Bryan Street. They lock up the slaves in the speculator jail when they brought them here to the auction. Most of the speculators come in the night before the sale and stop at the Pulaski House. The slaves was took to the pen under the hotel. [40]

Whilst us was all a-working away at house and yard jobs, the old folks would tell us about times before us was born. They said slave dealers used to come around with a big long line of slaves a-marching to where there was going to be a big slave sale. Sometimes they marched them here from as far as Virginia. Old folks said they had done been fetched to this country on boats. Them boats was painted red, real bright red, and they went plumb to Africa to get the Niggers. When they got there, they got off and left the bright red boats empty for a while. Niggers likes red, and they would get on them boats to see what them red things was. When the boats was full of them foolish Niggers, the slave dealers would sail off with them and fetch them to this country to sell them to folks what had plantations. Them slave sales was awful bad in some ways, because sometimes they sold mammies away from their babies and families got scattered. Some of them never knowed what comed of their brothers and sisters and daddies and mammies. [46]

I saw them selling slaves myself here in Augusta at the old market. They put them up on something like a table, bid them off just like you would do horses or cows. They was two men. I can recollect. I know one was called Mr. Tom Heckle. He used to buy slaves, speculating. The other was named Wilson. They would sell your mother from the children. That was the reason so many colored people married their sisters

[157]

and brothers, not knowing until they got to talking about it. One would say, "I remember my grandmother," and another would say, "That's *my* grandmother," and then they'd find out they were sister and brother.

Speculators used to steal children. I saw the wagons. They were just like the wagons that came from North Carolina with apples in. They had big covers on them. The speculators had plantations where they kept the children until they were big enough to sell, and they had an old woman there to tend to those children.[42]

WAR AND FREEDOM

The Northern soldiers come to town playing Yankee Doodle. When freedom come, they called all the white people to the courthouse first and told them the darkies was free. Then on a certain day they called all the colored people down to the parade ground. They had built a big stand, and the Yankees and some of our leading colored men got up and spoke, and told the Negroes: "You are free now. Don't steal. Now work and make a living. Do honest work. Make an honest living to support yourself and children. No more masters. You are free."

The slaves that was freed, and the country Negroes that had been run off, or had run away from the plantations, was staying in Augusta in government houses, great big old barns. They would all get free provisions from the Freedman's Bureau, but people like us, Augusta citizens, didn't get free provisions. We had to work. It spoiled some of them. When the smallpox come, they died up like hogs, all over Broad Street and everywhere.[42]

My mother said she prayed to the Lord not to let Niggers be slaves all their lives and sure enough the Yankees come and freed us. Some of the slaves shouted and hollered for joy when Miss Marion called us to-

gether and said us was free and wasn't slaves no more. Most of them went right out and left her and hired out to make money for themselves.[5]

When the war broke out my mistress's home became a sewing center and different women in the neighborhood would come there every day to make clothes for the soldiers. On each bed was placed the vests, coats, shirts, pants and caps. One group did all the cutting, one the stitching, and one the fitting. Many women cried while they sewed, heart-broken because their husbands and sons had to go to the war. One day the Yanks came to our plantation and took all of the best horses. In one of their wagons were bales of money which they had taken. Money then was blue in color, plus silver and gold. After taking the horses they drank as much whiskey as they could hold and then filled their canteens. The rest of the whiskey they filled with spit. The master didn't interfere for fear of the long guns which they carried.[18]

The first regiment of soldiers seemed to have darkened the sky. These soldiers ransacked the Browning home and found a buggy, a gun, and a baby go-cart. After breaking the buggy into pieces they broke the gun across the buggy wheels. They then gave me the baby cart telling me to ride my baby brother in it. They also searched for money and other valuables but the best goods including the piano were hid in the slave homes. The white families were aware of the fact that the Yankees would not bother the slave homes.[22]

The Yankees camped at Hawkinsville for a long time. I did hate them things and was scared to death of them. Our white folks had several houses on the back of the plantation where they kept corn and all kinds of rations. The Yankees come out to our place and went in them houses and took what they wanted. My mistress said she wasn't going to fool with them: they'd have to take what they wanted. She hid all her silver and jewelry when she heard they was in Macon. Whenever I seen

any of them coming to the plantation I run and hid or got with the white folks. Of course they never bothered nobody, but we was all scared. They took all the rations they wanted. There was many a glad soul when we heard they'd gone back home.[2]

The Yankees passed through and caught Ole Marse Jim and made him pull off his boots and run bare-footed through a cane brake with half a bushel of potatoes tied around his neck; then they made him put his boots back on and carried him down to the mill and tied him to the water post. They were getting ready to break his neck when one of Marster's slaves, Ole Peter Smith, asked them if they intended to kill Marse Jim, and when they said, "yes," Peter choked up and said, "Well, please sir, let me die with Ole Marse!" Well, them Yankees let Ole Marse loose and left![41]

During the war Mistress had one room all fixed up to take care of sick soldiers. They would come straggling in, all sick or shot, and sometimes we had a room full of them. Mistress had one young boy to do nothing but look after them and many a night I got up and held the candle for them to see the way to the room. I saw plenty of wounded soldiers. We are right on the road to Wrightsboro, and plenty of them pass by. That Confederate War was the terriblest, awfullest thing.

Nobody but me knowed where Mistress buried her gold money and finger rings and earrings and breast-pins. I held the candle then, too. Mistress and Marster (he was home then) and me went down back of the grape arbor to the garden house. Marster took up some planks, and he dug a hole like a grave and buried a big iron box with all them things in it; then he put back the planks. Nobody ever found them, and after the war was over we went and got them.[15]

I was fifteen years old when Marster came out in the fields and told them they were as free as he was. My family stayed with him. He gave

them a horse or mule, their groceries and a patch to work that they paid for in about three years time. Before the war whenever his slaves reached seventy years, the master set them free and gave them a mule, a cow and a patch. I can remember my grandmother and grandfather getting theirs.[44]

Times was hard during the war but from what I've heard the folks that was old folks then say they warn't near as bad here as in lots of other places. Sure, I can remember them Yankees coming here, but that was after the war was done over. Where they camped was mostly woods then, and their camp reached nearly all the way to where Milledge Avenue is now. Us chillun was scared to death of them soldiers and stayed out of their way all us could. My master, Mr. Stevens Thomas, hid all of his family's silver and other valuables that could be put out of sight, for them Yankees just went around taking whatever they wanted. They stole all kinds of food out of the homes, went into the smokehouses and got hams, and caught up the chickens. They just reached out and took what they wanted and laughed about it like they hadn't been stealing. Them Yankees brought the smallpox here with them and give it to all the Athens folks, and that was something awful. Folks just died out with it so bad.[45]

Why we didn't have no salt, just plain salt, and couldn't get none them days. We had to get up the dirt in the smokehouse where the meat had dripped and run it like lye, to get salt to put on things. Times was sure hard and our master was off in the war all four years, and we had to do the best we could. We Niggers wouldn't know nothing about it at all if it hadn't been for a little old black, sassy woman in the quarters that was a talking all the time about freedom. She give our white folks lots of trouble. She was so sassy to them, but they didn't sell her and she was set free along with us. When they all come home from the war

and Marster called us up and told us we was free, some rejoiced and shouted, but some didn't: they was sorry. Lewis, my husband, came a running over there and wanted me and the chillun to go over to his white folks' place with him, and I wouldn't go. I wouldn't leave my white folks. I told Lewis to go on and let me alone; I knowed my white folks and they was good to me, but in slavery. After a few years he finally persuaded me to go over to the Willis place and live with him, and his white folks was powerful good to me.[19]

I was too little to know much about the war, but little as I was, there's one thing that's still fresh in my memory now as then, and that's how people watched and waited to hear that old Georgia train come in. Not many folks was able to take the papers then, and the news in them was from one to two weeks old when they got here. All the men that was able to fight was off at the front and the folks at home was anxious for news. The way that old train brought them the news was like this: if the southern troops was in the front, then that old whistle just blowed continuously, but if it was bad news, then it was just one short, sharp blast. In that way, from the time it got in hearing, everybody could tell by the whistle if the news was good or bad and, believe me, everybody would listen to that train.[45]

I remember very clearly when Mr. Crowder gave his darkies their freedom. Marster sent me and my mammy out to the cabin to tell all the darkies to come up to the big house. When they got there, there were so many that some were up on the porch, on the steps and all over the yard. Mr. Crowder stood up on the porch and said, "You darkies are all free now. You don't belong to me no more. Now pack up your things and go on off." My Lord! How them darkies did bawl! And most of them did not leave Old Marster.[46]

One day us chillun was playing in the sand pile and us looked up and

seed a passel of Yankees coming. There was so many of them it was like a flock of bluebirds. Before they left some folks thought they was more like blue devils. My mammy was in the kitchen and Ole Miss said: "Look out of that window, Milly. The Yankees is coming for sure and they's going to free you and take you and your chillun away from me. Don't leave me! Please don't leave me, Milly!" Them Yankees swarmed into the yard. They opened the smokehouse, chicken yard, corn crib, and everything on the place. They took what they wanted and told us the rest was ours to do what us pleased with. They said us was free and that what was on the plantation belonged to us, then they went off and us never seed them no more. When the war was over Ole Miss cried and cried and begged us not to leave her, but us did.[47]

That morning in May I was wearing a sleeveless apron and they—Miss Fannie and Miss Ann—put a bag of gold and silver, and some old greenback Confederate money in my apron and told me to hold on to it. Miss Fannie and Miss Ann, both of them, patted me on the head and said: "Now be a good little girl and don't move." On came the Blue Coats. They went all over the house searching everything with their guns and swords shining and flashing. I was so scared the sweat was running down my face in streams. Bless your life! When they came to the bedroom where I was standing by a bed, holding that money inside my apron, they didn't even glance at me the second time. Little did they think that little slave girl had the money they were hunting for. After the Yankees were gone, I gave it all back to Miss Fannie, and she didn't give me the first penny.[48]

I remember seeing soldiers. They come here to the plantation about ten o'clock after they surrender. They was awful, some of them with legs off or arms off. The Niggers took all the mules and put them down in the sand field. Then they took all the womens and put them in the

chillun's house. And they left a guard there to stand over them, and tell him not to get off the foot. You know they didn't want put no temptation in the way of them soldiers.[49]

During the early part of the war Mr. Ross fought with the Confederates, leaving his young son Robert in charge of his affairs. The young master was very fond of horses and his favorite horse Bill was trained to do tricks. One of these was to lie down when tickled on his flanks. The Yankees visited the plantation and tried to take this horse. Robert, who loved him dearly, refused to dismount, and as they were about to shoot the horse beneath him, the slaves began to plead. They explained that the boy was kind to everyone and devoted to animals, and because of that he was allowed to keep his horse.[50]

Marster didnt't have but two boys and one of them got killed in the war. That sorely did hurt our good Old Marster, but that was the onliest difference the war made on our place. When it was over and they said us was free, all the slaves stayed right on with the master. That was all they knowed to do. Marster told them they could stay on just as long as they wanted to, and they was right there on that hill 'till Marster had done died out and gone to Glory.[30]

Niggers got so bad after they got their freedom that the Ku Kluxers come around and made them behave theirselves. One of them Kluxers come to our house and set down and talked to us about how us ought to act, and how us was going to have to do, if us expected to live and do well. Us always thought it was our own old master, all dressed up in them white robes with his face covered up, and talking in a strange, put-on voice. None of Marster's Niggers never left him for about two or three years.[2]

REFERENCES

1. George Eason, Forsyth. All references cited here are as complete as recorded in the documents of the Federal Writers' Project.
2. Anderson Furr, 298 West Broad Street, Athens. Interviewed by Sadie B. Hornsby.
3. Rhodus Walton, Lumpkin. Interviewed by Adella S. Dixon.
4. Melvin Smith. Interviewed by E. Watson, July 15, 1937.
5. Susan Castle, 1257 West Hancock Avenue, Athens. Interviewed by Sadie B. Hornsby.
6. Celestia Avery, LaGrange.
7. George Coulton, Cochran. Interviewed by E. Watson.
8. Jane Mickens Toombs, Wilkes County.
9. Marshall Butler, Wilkes County.
10. William Ward, Atlanta.
11. Lewis Favor, Atlanta. Interviewed by E. Driskell, January 29, 1937.
12. Julia Cole, 169 Yonah Street, Athens. Interviewed by Corry Fowler.
13. Easter Jackson. Interviewed by Lucile Bridges, August 11, 1936.
14. Estella Jones, 1430 Wrightsboro Road, Augusta. Interviewed by Louise Oliphant.
15. Ellen Clairbourn, 808 Campbell Street, Augusta.
16. John Cole, Billips Street, Athens.
17. Adeline Willis, Lexington Road, Washington.
18. Mariah Calloway, Wilkes County.
19. Adeline Willis, Lexington Road, Washington.
20. Julia Henderson, 1405 Jones Street, Augusta. Interviewed by Maude Barragan.
21. Sarah Virgil, Hawkinsville. Interviewed May, 1937.
22. George Washington Browning, Walton County. Interviewed by Minnie B. Ross, January 25, 1937.
23. Anonymous slave of John Hill, Madison.
24. Henry Rogers, Wilkes County.
25. Charlie Pye, Columbus.
26. Ellen Campbell, 1030 Brayton Street, Augusta. Interviewed by Ruby Lorraine Radford and Edith Bell Love.
27. W. B. Allen, 425 Second Avenue, Columbus. Interviewed by J. R. Jones, May 10, 1937.
28. William McWhorter, 383 West Broad Street, Athens. Interviewed by Sadie Hornsby, September 30, 1938.

29. Alec Pope, 1345 Rockspring Street, Athens. Interviewed by Sadie Hornsby, April 28, 1938.
30. Julia Larkin, 693 Meigs Street, Athens. Interviewed by Grace McCune.
31. Benjamin Johnston. Interviewed July 28, 1937.
32. Ferebe Rogers, Milledgeville. Interviewed by Ruth Chitty, December 9, 1936.
33. Squire Harris, 1407 Jones Street, Augusta. Interviewed by Maude Barragan, June 16, 1937.
34. Richard Orford, 54 Brown Avenue, Atlanta. Interviewed by E. F. Driskell, May 20, 1937.
35. Annie Price, Spaulding County. Interviewed January 20, 1937.
36. Hannah Murphy, Augusta. Interviewed by Maude Barragan.
37. Mary Ferguson, 1928 Oak Avenue, Columbus. Interviewed December 18, 1936.
38. Amelia Dorsey, 1034 Phelps Street, Augusta. Interviewed by Maude Barragan, September 28, 1936.
39. Mollie Kensey, Washington, Georgia. Interviewed by Geneva Tonsell, November, 1939.
40. George Carter.
41. Paul Smith, 429 China Street, Athens. Interviewed by Grace McCune.
42. Eugene Wesley Smith, 1105 Robert Street, Augusta. Interviewed by Maude Barragan.
43. Charlie Tye Smith, East Solomon Avenue, Locust Grove. Interviewed by Mary A. Crawford, September 16, 1936.
44. Mollie Mitchell, 507 East Chappell Street, Griffin. Interviewed by Alberta Minor, October 5, 1936.
45. Ike Derricotte, 554 Hancock Avenue, Athens. Interviewed by Grace McCune, August 19, 1938.
46. Lewis Ogletree, 501 East Tinsley Street, Griffin. Interviewed by Mary Crawford, August 21, 1936.
47. Alice Green, 156 Willow Street, Athens. Interviewed by Sadie B. Hornsby, July 8, 1938.
48. Mary Colbert, 168 Pearl Street, Athens. Interviewed by Sadie B. Hornsby.
49. Rachel Sullivan, 1327 Reynolds Street, Augusta. Interviewed by Ruby Lorraine Radford and Edith Bell Love.
50. Della Briscoe, Macon. Interviewed by Adella S. Dixon, 1937.

INDEX

Ronald Killion teaches at Limestone College, Gaffney, South Carolina. Charles Waller teaches at the University of Georgia, Athens. The original interviews which make up *Slavery Time When I Was Chillun down on Marster's Plantation* are preserved at The University of Georgia Library, Special Collections. The illustrations have been reproduced from Rudolf Eickemeyer, *Down South*, New York, 1900. § This book has been planned and edited at Savannah, Georgia, by The Beehive Press which publishes sources and studies of southern history and literature. Its pressmark, which appears above and pictures bees busy at their hive, expresses the enthusiasm of this work; the source of the pressmark— an early colonial pamphlet entitled *An Impartial Enquiry into the State and Utility of the Province of Georgia*, London, 1741—suggests a spirit of free intellectual endeavor. § This book was printed by The Stinehour Press at Lunenburg, Vermont.

THE BEEHIVE PRESS
321 Barnard Street · Savannah · Georgia 31401